# In
# Everness

## Smita Jayakar

VETERAN BOLLYWOOD ACTRESS
& SPIRITUAL HEALER
BASED ON TRUE LIFE EVENTS

Become
Shakespeare
.com

First published in 2018 by

Becomeshakespeare.com

Wordit Content Design & Editing Services Pvt Ltd
Unit - 26, Building A -1, Nr Wadala RTO,
Wadala (East), Mumbai 400037, India
T: +91 8080226699

**ISBN - 978-93-88081-45-0**

## ACKNOWLEDGMENTS

I thank my family, friends and acquaintances for their support and love through my entire journey and their help in bringing this book together.

I am deeply grateful to my editor Prakriti Venkatesh for her conscientious effort to understand and comprehend my thought process and also in helping structure my diverse thoughts into composite messages with her artful way with words. It was a pleasure working with her.

Many thanks to Vidya Heble for her assistance with the final proof reading process.

Also, much thanks to my publishing team for their efforts in working up a brilliant layout that augments the message I wish to convey through 'In Everness.'

## ABOUT THE AUTHOR

SMITA JAYAKAR has led both an ordinary and extraordinary life. As a veteran actress, Smita is a known and recognized face and has been appreciated for her skills as a fine actor, in cinema, television and theatre. But there is a facet beyond her well-known self that Smita has been working on over the past 30 years. Exploring and self experimenting with various techniques of Holistic Healing, Smita has succeeded in evolving simple teachings and principles to help people live life to the fullest. In every activity, her focus has been observing the human spirit and its workings.

**'In Everness'** has been born from research, observation, experiences and Smita's own spiritual journey. Though she loves to call herself spiritual, Smita clarifies that spirituality stands apart, with or sans religion. What she has developed is a simple and effective technique to be peaceful and happy, that can be applied to all individuals regardless of religion, caste or creed. After extensive research, study and exhaustive observation, Smita affirms that there is a spiritual being in each of us, waiting to be tapped by the self. She feels that there are a few basic steps that can simplify and decomplicate life for each individual if they have the patience and capacity to understand and apply these principles effectively in day-to-day living.

Smita Jayakar has already published her book 'Before Tomorrow' that encompasses her entire life journey and how her ordinary life has been transformed into extraordinary by applying simple principles of Spirituality in practical life.

In addition to her books, Smita is a contributing editor in the newspaper segment, The Speaking Tree, and a regular with articles in life magazines.

Smita is also an accomplished motivational speaker and Reiki Grandmaster. She is a Pranic Healer and has certificates of achievement from CHII (California Hypnosis Institute of India). However, Smita's area of expertise lies in Chakra Healing. She has done in-depth study and research on 'Aligning Energy Centres of the Body to enhance life skills' and conducts workshops and seminars with private groups, college students, business professionals and non-profit organisations. Smita is available for public speaking events, seminars and teleconferences, and personal healing sessions. She can be reached at www.newleaftrust.com or via email at trust.newleaf@gmail.com or at www.facebook/smitajayakar.

**'I explore so I learn, I learn so I share, I share so I am'**

I have been a keen observer since childhood and my passion has been to pursue what I call, 'Human Study', a term that has drawn me towards exploring myself and each individual who steps into my life, as they are, in their own unique characteristic capacity. So far, all my learning has originated from interesting interactions and conversations that have led to deeper observation and research.

**'In Everness'** is an after-effect of many such stimulating exchanges. Interestingly, after I wrote my first book, 'Before Tomorrow', people began approaching me, trying to raise doubts on how a worldly being like me, an actress who was in one of the most attractive professions, could switch track and turn to 'Spirituality' and give up all the pleasures that life had to offer. That is when the idea of my second book struck.

I began to ponder over why most people shy away from the word **'Spirituality'**. Through all the opinions I gathered, it became certain that Spirituality is one concept that has been misconstrued, misinterpreted and misunderstood beyond belief. In my second book, I have decided at the least to try and demystify the concept of Spirituality, also refuting notions that have been linked to Spirituality for no reason whatsoever.

The term 'Spiritually inclined' has become a fad today. Most people I meet use this term without understanding the basics of it. They try and meditate through various techniques, go for pilgrimages, head to yoga camps, lock themselves out at remote getaways far off from external chaos - but does all this really typify Spirituality?

To be precise, if I speak by experience, all this might guide you towards Spirituality but the concept itself is much, much simpler than all of this. **Spirituality is awareness, comprehension, and a simple effort of being and staying YOU, right here, right now, in this very worldly existence.** The Universe has wonderfully equipped each one of us with all the resources we need to enjoy a good life. All we need is a change in perspective.

This is where Spirituality helps. Spirituality is the art of internal transformation to alter the self. It is the art of acceptance, to take situations, problems and criticalities in life as mere happenings, to stop attaching strings, to stop complaining and struggling to change everything around. It is the slow process of cultivating internal happiness so the quality of life can improve. It is the conscious effort of harnessing your mind power so you can think positive and take affirmative action.

Today, with personal, professional and social lives becoming more complex, the need for deciphering the Buddha within us has become the need of the hour, more of a necessity than a luxury. **'In Everness'** is a realistic effort to suggest ways to decode this tiny Buddha who lies latent inside each one of us.

At this point, I would humbly want to admit that I do not say any of this as a spiritual guru, preacher or master, but as another fellow human who has learnt out of experience and exploration. My intent through **'In Everness'** is to share my learnings on how you can cultivate and direct the immense powers of your mind, body and soul to achieve greater success, both in the internal and external worlds.

I firmly believe that once you are able to balance your internal energies, prosperity and abundance will flow. I hope and pray that each one of you gathers much out of these practical tips for designing finer life journeys ahead.

# CHAPTERS

~ Divine Friend Dadashreeji ~

|| ॐ ज्योतिरुपाय परमसखाय परमानंदाय दादाश्रीजी नमो नमः ||

|| Aum Jyotiroopaay Paramsakhaay Parmaanandaay
Dadashreeji Namo Namah ||

Meaning of Dadashreeji mantr:
*He Whose form is Light*
*And Who is Supreme Friend*
*And His quality is Supreme Bliss*
*To That Dadashreeji we offer obeisance multiple times.*

*"I am neither a mystic nor a fortune-teller, neither a saint nor a sage; I am not a Guru, Master or God. Do not categorize me in any of this. I am just you, your higher sacred self."*

— **Dadashreeji**

# CHAPTER 1
## MY LIVING INSPIRATION

———————◆◆◆———————

As I move ahead in my attempt to unravel the mysteries and strengths of the human mind and soul through my second book, **'In Everness'**, I would like to dedicate every word of it to my inspiration, my motivation, and my living spiritual guide, **Dadashreeji**.

As reflected beautifully through his quote, Dadashreeji does not like to brand himself as a saint or master, but prefers being referred to as **'Love Incarnate'**. The simplicity, charisma and dynamism of this young divine friend is what pulled me to him and today is slowly pulling thousands from across the globe to work with him on his mission – of combining practical intelligence with deep spiritual insight and knowledge to live full, meaningful lives, with positivity, compassion and love.

After having interacted with a number of spiritual leaders, gurus and masters through the many years of my spiritual journey, Dadashreeji fascinated me most because he is a young professional who has consciously, out of choice, diverted his energies towards helping people demystify spirituality. It has also been amazing to see how he is able to convey deep spiritual messages in very simple ways, making them easy to understand and follow. He does not envelop his words in heavy jargon and terminology. Another aspect that has attracted me towards Dadashreeji is that he was a medical practitioner who spent years observing and understanding the workings of the human body and then moved deeper to correlate it to the exploration of how the human mind, body and soul function together.

Moving through his medical profession, Dadashreeji realized that he could only cure people of their physical ailments and relieve external pain, but he strongly felt the need to heal people from the inside. That is when his quest for the ultimate truth began. In the years that followed, Dada began to meditate, read and explore the mystery, power and beauty that lay hidden in the human soul. He had strange visions of saints, historical figures and deities. Finally, in year 2006, The Great Yogi Mahavataar Babaji appeared before Dadashreeji and revealed, "My consciousness is within you to help your mission of Maitri or Friendship, as The Love Incarnate." After this mystical encounter, Dadashreeji spent a few years on his journey within, exploring his origin, and realizing the true purpose of his coming. He examined the human mind and the cause of all suffering from a spiritual perspective. Enlightened by his learnings, Dadashreeji took on the role of a **'Divine Friend'**, embarking on his journey of rendering selfless social and spiritual service to mankind.

Dadashreeji founded the **MaitriBodh Parivaar** in 2013 to mobilize like-minded volunteers, spiritual seekers, students and professionals to serve humanity selflessly. MaitriBodh Parivaar's work is aimed at transforming humanity through self-realization, preparing it to enter the new era of universal love and peace. Each member of the MaitriBodh Parivaar shares a mission - to develop, nurture and strengthen the bond of human love and friendship. The Parivaar that began with merely 7 Mitras now runs into thousands, spanning **India, Moscow, Germany, Russia, Europe, Australia and the UK.**

Beyond his effort of bringing about positive transformation in each member of the MaitriBodh family through his **Personal Transformation or Bodh programs**, Dadashreeji also aims at raising **Social Consciousness** levels, changing people's approach and perception towards society as a whole.

MBP has launched numerous **social upliftment and development programs** for women, children, the aged and the youth for bringing greater harmony between the self, home, community, and the world. Keeping up his commitment towards building a better tomorrow, Dadashreeji has also set in motion several projects for **Education and Environmental protection**. Within a few years of its establishment, the MaitriBodh Parivaar has grown and expanded appreciably, extending its reach to around **15 countries across the globe**.

For me, it has been an enlightening experience to meet a living disciple of the Great Guru Mahavataar Babaji whom I had been wanting to know more about, ever since I read about him in Paramahansa Yogananda's captivating book *Autobiography of a Yogi.* Beyond his spiritual persona, it has been wonderful to come across a young spiritual guide like Dadashreeji who has sharpness, clarity of thought and who professes practical action for personal and social development and reform.

Today, as I begin my second book, it is extremely important to mention that Dadashreeji is one guide who has made me understand the true, practical meaning of Spirituality and clarified that this understanding needs to be put to use in everyday being to chart a better, more peaceful and meaningful life journey ahead.

Dadashreeji, I thank you whole-heartedly for having shown me a clear path so I can share the knowledge I have been so fortunate to gather during the course of this lifetime.

*"We are not human beings having a spiritual experience.
We are spiritual beings having a human experience."*

**— Pierre Teilhard de Chardin**

# Chapter 2
## Applied Spirituality

———— ◆◆◆ ————

This quote has fascinated me as much as inspired me to move ahead on my quest for finding a deeper meaning in life. But this is probably one quote that is very hard to relate to.

Why, you may ask? It's simply because despite so much activity oriented around Spirituality, most of us are still struggling for answers to very basic questions like "What is Spirituality?", "Am I Spiritual?", "Do I have time to practice Spirituality between my busy schedules?"," I don't really pray every day, so no chance I can be Spiritual" or "Would people laugh at me if I were to say that I am Spiritual?"

It is interesting to note that till date no book or reference site can give you a clear definition of what Spirituality means. Though traditionally, spirituality refers to a process of re-formation of the personality, there is no single, widely-agreed-upon definition of spirituality. So at the outset I will try and lay out my understanding of Spirituality, what it means to me, how it has been misread and misinterpreted, and what Spirituality by and large entails.

When I began to explore Spirituality, I came across varied definitions and readings on the word "Spirituality", making my probing mind even more inquisitive. But I was no enlightened preacher who could decipher messages easily so I decided to gather more. Slowly and steadily as I began to read, discuss, confer, argue and analyze, it became clear that there was no right or wrong approach to Spirituality. I also realized that Spirituality was a very broad concept with room for many perspectives.

So I decided to simplify things for myself. I began to work on something termed 'Applied Spirituality' – Spirituality that I could practise on a day-to-day basis and relate to, on ways how I could make Spirituality work for me between my busy shooting schedules and how I could take the help of Spirituality in making my life happier and content, both personally and professionally.

After all my research, study and understanding, I chalked out a few learnings that I would like to share with you.

Spirituality requires no special effort to be understood or practised; it just needs basic belief in one beautiful, inclusive universe.

❦

It is essential to understand that life is not divided into the "spiritual" and "non-spiritual". Everything in life — all of its moments, events, circumstances, situations, and interactions — are part of what "spirituality" is.

❦

Spirituality needs no external changes, either in your surroundings or in your lifestyle. You can be spiritual, working in a hectic 8-10 job or even as you sip your favourite wine and whisky. What you need is internal change and a change in perspective.

❦

Spirituality means inculcating the capacity of being and staying you under all circumstances, whether in anger, grief, pressure or merriment.

❦

Spirituality can be experienced differently by each
individual even in simple everyday activities,
at office or home.

Spirituality does not need you to necessarily follow
any particular routine or schedule like meditating
for a certain period or doing daily yoga, though
these activities can surely help in pacifying the
mind and improving focus.

Spirituality can be experienced even while
spending time with your loved ones on an outing
or enjoying any form of creative expression.

It is as important to understand that just because
you become spiritual, all your problems and
woes will not vanish. However, be assured that
the change in perspective will help you glide
through any life test comfortably.

As an artist who stays busy 365 days of the year, I have realized that in today's day and age where life is busy and time is running fast, it is crucial for each one of us to try and touch base with Spirituality so we stay rooted and calm. I speak more for highly educated, sharp and motivated professionals who have often walked up to me after my seminars asking extremely pertinent questions. But it has been surprising to note that beyond the sense of not having understood the concept of Spirituality, most people I interact with carry brilliantly erroneous notions about Spirituality.

The most common misrepresentation is regarding Spirituality and Religion. For most people, spirituality is seen as practically equivalent to religion. They feel that only believers can experience Spirituality. Conversely, if someone is a non-believer, the spiritual experience must be alien to them, something they can't possibly understand. But there is nothing that could be further from the truth. The spiritual experience is human and one can feel it without the slightest belief in any religion or ritual. Love, beauty, friendship, the exploration of the self - none of these things requires religion. Nor do they require any religious identity.

For some people, spirituality is all about devotion to a religious faith. Others seek a more broad-based definition for the term. In my belief, it is wrong to brand either as the correct analysis of Spirituality.

In this case, I would rather say, to each his own. Whatever works for you to bring peace of mind and enhance the quality of life is good.

Though I am a firm believer in God, for me, spirituality and religion are interconnected at a deeper level but at the practical level, they stand way apart. Spirituality focuses on harnessing humanistic qualities such as love, compassion, patience, tolerance, forgiveness, contentment and harmony, rather than any ritualistic dealing. It is more a personal relationship with the energy of the universe, the love that surrounds us all but which we fail to recognize, and the attempt to go with the inner good self.

Spirituality is not the inevitability of pain or the evasion of consequences or errors, but the art of learning how to live with them in a conscious way. Practicing Spirituality takes time and effort but as the heart opens up, relationships - personal, professional and with the self - get smoother and better. I say this going purely by personal experience and I speak as a seeker, not a preacher. I have seen practical changes happening inside and around me with mere mental effort, so I say Spirituality works.

Spirituality has a lot to it but here are a few of my readings on what Spirituality really entails. I will deal with each of these topics in an in-depth manner in the chapters that follow.

## BE AND STAY YOU

To be spiritual is to be in conscious connection with one's true nature; to be self-aware. Believe it or not, there is a universal spiritual teaching which is already engrained in each one of us when we step into this so-called mortal world. It's like a chip that has been pre-fitted into our brainwave networks. It's just that over a period of time, due to our survival instincts and our amazing capability to complicate, this chip loses its edge. That is probably when spirituality steps in. And what does it suggest? Well simply, to make the mind clear, more alert and less complicated. We are all driven by situations, set ups and circumstances. Even the most patient people tend to lose control when faced with tough situations. So does that mean that if you practice Spirituality, you do not react? The suggestion is that **YOU ACT, BUT DO NOT REACT**.

When faced with a tough situation, many of us often blow up and forget what to do next. This in fact has a snowball effect and negatively affects all other actions that follow. Even though the situation might die down, the after-effects still linger. Basically, none of us like being angry, unhappy or upset but the situation forces us to react. Spiritual teaching calls for making your mind aware that it basically wants to stay happy, in all situations and at all times, and reiterating this assertion a few times every day. This slow process will lessen the negativity that erupts out of each situation and reduce instances. Even when a situation arises, the suggestion is to take a second off and think of focused action rather than a stark reaction. Then there will be no problems, just situations to respond to and your response will be conscious, appropriate and empowered. This process will take time and effort but trust me, it will work in the long run.

## ENJOY IN THE PRESENT

You do not have to climb high mountains or cut yourself off from the world or give away all your possessions to be Spiritual. All you need to do is live in the present, not the past or the future because one is gone and the other is unpredictable. When you are in the present, you are free of the limitations of the past and anxiety about the future. As you deepen into presence, you will experience a completely different dimension of yourself and of life. You will discover that you are empowered from within and you exist in the realization of oneness. You will stop being concerned with judgments, opinions and expectations of others. Your life will gradually transform and all these qualities of presence will flow into your day-to-day life and relationships.

## BE AWARE

It is very easy to sit in peaceful meditation for hours and hours, day after day, if you were to not get up and face the duties of the day. But the challenge for each of us is to remain conscious and aware when the mind and emotions are trying to run havoc. Spiritual practice calls for you to simply remain aware of where you are and what you are feeling – whether it be happiness, sadness, anger, guilt, stress or love. There could be an emotional, professional or personal disturbance in the mind. Don't try and shut down the emotion or thought because it will come back more strongly. Just hold on to the awareness of the problem without trying to attach any more meaning or emotion to it or reliving the scenario. This will help you find a solution to the problem in a more practical way. The process will have to be a slow one but as you become more alert and aware of each and every moment and everything around you, life situations will seem easier to handle.

## DON'T AVOID ACTION

If you are in a situation that is causing you to be unhappy, even if you are conscious and trying to dissolve the arising emotion, this will never be enough if there is some action that you should be taking but are not, for whatever reason. Avoiding taking action simply means more emotion is being created.

So, as well as being conscious and aware, especially when times are difficult, you have to take assertive action. It may be a phone call, a letter, looking something up, even having a difficult conversation, or making a huge life change. Whatever it is, until the intention is in place to take the required action, the emotion will remain. As the emotion starts getting stronger, at some point there will be the knowledge as to what action needs to be taken in order to resolve the situation. Do not avoid taking that action, because it is essential for your peace of mind.

## OBSERVE

It is easy to get caught up in the chaotic rhythm of our daily lives and routines. Although challenging at first, attempt to observe yourself as you move through your day. Set an intention to pause some time of the day to observe your breath, actions, interactions with others, and your inner dialogue with yourself. This is especially helpful in moments of stress or difficulty. Instead of getting attached or judging your thoughts, simply notice them.

Spend more time observing nature. Look around as you walk outside. This conscious observation can begin to shift your perspective. Instead of looking at the day as something to just "get through," you can begin to step out of the chronic state of busyness and appreciate a deeper experience of each moment as more interesting and enjoyable.

## CHANGE YOURSELF FOR YOURSELF

It is one thing to read, research and analyze aspects of Spirituality, and another to make Spirituality work for you. If you want to transform your life, focus on trying to mirror the learnings in your own life, personality traits and relationships. Always remember that unless you change, nothing around you will change. When you read about forgiveness, don't think about others who need to learn to forgive you; think instead about whom you can forgive. Forgive for yourself, not for others. When you understand Spiritual practices, first think about how it can improve life situations for you rather than thinking about how someone else needs to learn more than you. Transform for yourself and others will transform with you.

## MAKE CHANGES SLOWLY

This is probably the most important learning amongst all the takeaways of Spirituality. A lot of people I meet have great intentions of changing their life and are super-enthusiastic for a while, and then stop. Much like all else, if you want long-term change in your life, you have to start slowly, knowing that the initial spurt of energy won't last. Instead, aim at changing habits. Once a new habit is formed, it can carry your practice when the initial enthusiasm is gone. The habit will stabilize your practice, enabling inspiration to stay within it.

In this test of life, you can excel in your personal and professional relationships but this will require focus and determination. If you do make up your mind to transform, transformation will happen.

*"What the hell is instant? Nothing is instant"*

— **John Green**

CHAPTER 3
THE AGE OF INSTANTS

W e are all living in a fast paced world where most things we practice run around the clock. Our everyday life is practically slotted and scheduled according to perfect timetables. The most precious possession today beyond money is 'TIME'. Struggling to keep pace, we have all got accustomed to a unique concept called 'Instants'. From noodles to pizzas, from messaging to online results and deliveries, we want everything instantly.

So most people I meet expect the same from their Spiritual practices – INSTANT RESULTS. They want to get as much as possible, as quickly as possible, from as little commitment as possible. I have had some interesting episodes during my workshops when people walk up to me trying to comprehend why meditation does not work for them. Surprisingly when I ask how long they have been practicing mediation, the answers do not move beyond a few days to maybe a month. Common concerns are also regarding whether they have got their meditation practices right because meditation seems to be yielding no RESULTS.

Well, let me clarify here that even the most progressed masters have not been able to invent an instant technique that can make spirituality work for you. There are various methodologies, techniques and even extremely less time-consuming methods to reach your spiritual goals, provided there is patience and persistence. Through experience, I can say that each of us can surely pull time out between our busy schedules to focus on inner happenings, provided you have the intent. However, be rest assured that there will be no instant results.

Think about it. Does nature follow shortcuts? There is clearly a season for all things. Every plant blossoms and bears fruit when the time is right and not one instant before. The same concept applies to us humans, especially when it comes to a phenomenon like Spirituality. All of us can become finer human beings and achieve greater success if we have patience, dedication and faith.

With our professional lives being performance-driven, we all feel a need to accomplish something.

We're always trying to reach the finish line so that we can feel a sense of completion and move onto something else. However, meditation and spirituality are never quite like that. Spirituality is a process, not an event. It involves long-term changes in your thinking, your perspective and your lifestyle. It is important that if you want to change, it has to be in slow degrees. You cannot change habits and lifestyles overnight, so move at a relaxed and steady pace.

At this stage I would also want to reiterate that contrary to the commonly-held notion, Spirituality does not necessarily involve a lot of ritualistic dealings and routines or schedules, though a common practice for increasing focus, concentrating on the inner self and calming the mind can surely help. Again, the options are open. One can take up meditation in any form, take up regular chanting, do a bit of yoga, or just sit peacefully for a few minutes at the end of day, focusing attention on the happenings of the day and let thoughts flow freely. There are no set formulas for deciding your spiritual practice. Anything that works for you and helps you increase focus and reduce mental disturbance is good.

However, before you set out to choose any technique, it is vital that you ask yourself a few questions. Answers to these will help you streamline your thought process and formulate a practice that you will be able to follow for a long term.

*What are your worldly obligations?*

We are all tied down by our daily chores and activities that require us to devote time and energy. And though we may daydream of cutting ourselves off from all responsibility, it is out of the realm of possibility. It is crucial to understand that without fulfilling our worldly obligations, we will neglect to establish a solid foundation upon which we can build our spiritual lives. It is as important to take care of daily chores and errands, as of our body, hygiene, of good sleep and of worldly priorities as much as of our spiritual growth, because both are inseparably intertwined.

*What are your personal priorities?*

Each one of us has unique hobbies, likes and personal relaxation techniques. Some people I speak to enjoy sport activities, some crafts, some cooking, some partying and some simply spending time with family. Well, I would suggest that you make time for relaxing and enjoying with these personal pastimes before deciding on a practice.

*What would be the focus of your daily practice?*

I would again say that anything that gives you peace of mind and makes you happy would be good enough as a daily practice. Some people have no need for any type of daily ritual, other people like doing a bit of daily meditation, yoga or prayer. It's up to you to determine what exactly you find yourself doing every day and what you need to be doing every day.

❈

*What do you have time for?*

Once you have a fair idea of what daily practice helps you, it is important that you make time for it every day, even if that means shortening or lengthening your practice. When you have little time, you can do only a little; when you have more time, you can do more. It's that simple. Within the time you can afford, fit what you absolutely need to do but make it regular.

❈

*When are you most comfortable doing the practice?*

Many of my friends prefer to do their spiritual practice at night when they're relaxing after work, while I've always been a morning person and get my best work done before I leave my house. Biasing your practice towards a particular time of the day can benefit your practice substantially, but if you don't have such a preference, using any available time works just as well.

❈

While each of us will need to chalk out our own path and roadmap to spiritual growth, throughout what we do, the focus will have to be on enhancing humanistic qualities of love, compassion, patience, tolerance, forgiveness, contentment and harmony in thought and deed. Harnessing these qualities will require a lot more patience and practise than following a daily routine. The first hurdle of confronting your ego and acknowledging your shortcomings will be the toughest to cross. Once your mind becomes open and accepting, you will slowly become non-judgemental about yourself and others. You will have better control over anger and aggression. Your thought process will become clearer and you will be able to take practical decisions and carry out required action rather than reacting to situations and problems. This in turn will give you the strength to face life situations more intelligently and strengthen relationships, both personal and professional.

Slowly you will evolve in a way where your internal and external life will be completely transformed. But the process will not be easy. There will be many stages to your spiritual evolution and many hurdles to cross. In my next chapter, I will talk about another major hurdle you will need to cross over for harnessing inner peace – STRESS.

*"It's not stress that kills us, it is our reaction to it"*

— **Hans Selye**

## Chapter 4
## Stress Redefined...

——————◆◆◆——————

Stress is a word that most of us use in common parlance. With limited understanding, we all assume that stress is either situational or incident-driven. We tend to think that modern times are full of stress, that what we face every day even within our daily routines and responsibilities contributes to stress.

At home, outside the house, within our personal and professional circles, we find a thousand causes of stress. But have any of us ever cared to find out what 'Stress' really means? Maybe very few of us would even want to know. But it is crucial to understand the true meaning of stress before we try and analyze stressors and find ways to relieve stress.

On a theoretical level, stress is a state of psychological and physiological imbalance resulting from the disparity between situational demand and the individual's ability and motivation to meet those needs. But you would be surprised to know that the roots of stress go deeper than just causes and occurrences. All emphasis is laid on the symptoms of stress but not the root cause, thus leaving its cure elusive.

Generally, most people use the word stress to refer to negative experiences. However, thinking about stress as exclusively something negative is a false impression. If I were to put it practically, Stress is our reaction to a changing, demanding environment. Properly considered, stress is really more about our capacity to handle change than it is about whether that change makes us feel good or bad. Change happens all the time, in personal relationships and work life, so it is important that we learn to handle stress in a suitable manner.

Stress is primarily based on perceptions, fears and anxieties. It is how one perceives a given situation or task. It is not what is actually happening, but a person's perception of what is happening. So the way we respond to any situation will lead us towards a stressful or a stress-free outcome.

Believe it or not, directing our thoughts in the right manner can make any situation, whether on the personal or professional front, stress-free.

Imagine a situation where nothing in life causes you any stress or excitement. You may become totally bored or may not be driven to live up to your potential. Some life changes such as joining a new job, getting married, or studying to master a new skill are positive and life-enhancing events, even though they can also be quite stressful. The stress generated out of these situations often pushes one to perform better. Even short-term stress, like getting set for an important job presentation, test, interview, or event gives you extra energy to do your best. This stress is termed Eustress or Positive stress. On the other front is Distress or extreme and long-term stress. This kind of negative stress needs attention because it can affect your physical and mental state, leaving you unable to concentrate or think clearly.

There are tips and tricks to gently tackle all forms of stress, whether short term or long term, which I will detail later in the chapter. But let's start by understanding what really causes 'Stress'?

Identifying what may be causing you stress is often the first step in learning how to better deal with it. Let me try and broadly define the most common sources of stress.

—► Environmental Stress ◄—

This is a response to things around you that cause stress, such as noise, crowding, and pressure from work or family. Even routine hassles such as getting the family out of the door in the morning, or dealing with a difficult co-worker, contribute to this stress. Long-term stressors such as dealing with a chronic disease, or caring for a child or sick family member, also come under this category. Identifying these stressors and learning to avoid them or deal with them will help lower your stress level.

### —— Social Stress ——

Each of us plays multiple social roles as parent, spouse, caregiver or employee. Each of these roles also comes with its own set of demands. Most often, social stressors include deadlines, financial problems, job interviews, disagreements, demands for your time and attention or co-parenting. With aspirations and desires continually rising, the skill of dealing with social stressors needs to be honed.

### —— Physical Stress or Fatigue ——

This kind of stress builds up over a long time and can take a hard toll on your body. It can be caused by working too much at your job or home. It can also be caused by not knowing how to manage your time well or how to take time out for rest and relaxation.

## ➤ Internal Stress ◄

Sometimes, you might have caught yourself worrying about things you can do nothing about or worrying for no reason at all. This is internal stress. Internal stress is when people make themselves stressed. This often happens when we worry about things we can't control or put ourselves in situations we know will cause us stress. Some people become addicted to the kind of hurried, tense, lifestyle that results from being under stress. They even look for stressful situations and feel stress about things that aren't stressful. It is more than important to understand and manage this kind of stress.

Though different people may experience the same type of events, each of them will experience that event in a unique way. Some people are more vulnerable to becoming stressed out than others in any given situation. An event like getting stuck in traffic might cause one person to become very stressed out while it might not affect another person much. Even with good stressors such as getting married, some individuals become highly anxious while others remain calm and composed.

How vulnerable you are personally to becoming stressed depends on a variety of factors, including your biological makeup, your perception of your ability to cope with challenges, and the intensity, timing, and duration of a stressful event. While some of these factors are not under your control, your reaction to most stressful situations is workable. Apart from understanding what really causes you stress, it is essential to recognize and accept that you are stressed, and work out ways to manage stress.

Well, you've recognized you are stressed, but what can you do now? Let me take you through a set of short- and long-term strategies for breaking through stress, that have worked very well for me and most of my acquaintances and friends. Hope they work for you.

## QUICK FIXES

One of the most immediate and easiest ways to deal with stress, whether at home or work is responding to your body's physical symptoms. Sometimes this can be as easy as stopping what you're doing and taking a few deep, relaxing breaths. Try it.

*The kids or any family member getting on your nerves?* Just step out of the situation. Go into another room or even the bathroom to get away! Shut the door. Take a few deep breaths. Experience the quiet. Feel the tension go out of your head, neck and shoulders and then get back.

*Having a bad day at work? Tensions mounting with your boss or colleague?*
Shut the door to your office if you have one and take a few minutes for yourself. If you share a cubicle, no problem either. Stroll down the hall, rinse your face with cool water or head outside for a few breaths of fresh air. Just getting away for a few minutes helps your mind calm down and helps you relax.

*Have a deadline to meet for report submission and still too much to read?*
Take a break. Push back from your desk. Roll your head and shoulders. Rub your hands together quickly to warm them and place them over your weary eyes, or just close your eyes and let your face and neck relax. Breathe in and out deeply. You have already lowered your stress and your blood pressure in just a few seconds.

Responding to the immediate physical effects of stress can help lessen the long-term and mental effects of stress. Developing a healthier lifestyle and building activities into your schedule that help you relax can also help your body and mind bounce back from stress.

Let's now move on to some long-term stress-busters.

## LONG-TERM STRATEGIES

I would lie if I say that I have never been stressed. Each of us gets stressed out from time to time. Striking a balance between work and home, making kids do well in a growing competitive environment, exhausting travel, work life and relationship challenges, worry has become the common habitual response to problems for all of us, leading to accumulated stress. However, like much else, there are extremely workable strategies to get rid of long term stress, provided you make up your mind to do so. Here are a few stress-busting strategies that work really well.

### IDENTIFY YOUR STRESSORS

A lot of the time, we all tend to gloss over our problems expecting them to vanish one fine day - but that never happens. In fact, the more you try and ignore a problem, the more it bothers you. If something is bothering you, even the smallest of things, identify what it is. If you think it should not be bothering you, stop and analyze why it does. Often, small irritants are indicators to larger issues that are bothering you but which you might be trying to cover up. Take time to identify the serious stressors in your life. This will help you understand that trivial stressors are not worth wasting time and energy on and, help you focus on facing up and managing serious stressors in life.

## RECOGNIZE WHAT YOU CAN CHANGE

This understanding is most important when it comes to stress at your work place or in professional circles. Before getting stressed about any issue, ask yourself this question – Can I change what is bothering me?

If yes, do not let the solutions remain at thought level, but take proactive steps to change or alter the situation. If you are stressed about your work profile and need clarity on your role and job responsibility, do not keep contemplating what is expected of you. Wait for an opportune moment to go and discuss it with your boss or superior. Also understand that the response may not always be favorable so be ready to take the alternate step.

When you realize that you cannot change a situation, be sensible and practical enough to change your response to the problem.

## REDUCE THE INTENSITY OF YOUR REACTIONS
## AND FOCUS ON A SOLUTION

Quite a few times, we tend to over-react to situations and instances, creating stress for ourselves. It is natural to react instantaneously but you have to learn not to let that reaction affect you long-term. As a strategy, whenever any situation looks out of control, try and pull yourself away, take a deep breath and walk out of the room. Once you step off, think rationally and accept the fact that no one is perfect, including your co-worker, your child, your parent, your partner or you. This thought itself will solve half the problem. Rather than wasting your time, attention and energy on the situation or instance, try and divert that energy to work out a solution that will benefit you and, in the process, others around you.

## SPELL OUT YOUR PRIORITIES AND
## OBLIGATIONS

Are you trying to be all things to all people? It is great to be helpful and nice, provided you are not being too harsh on yourself. Sometimes in trying too hard to do good for others, we don't do well for ourselves. Chalk out your priorities and obligations in life, but don't forget to tag yourself as one of those priorities.

Is working overtime every day worth the quality time you're sacrificing with your family and friends? Can't take an hour out of your busy week to relax and read your favourite book, but find yourself volunteering to help every family member, friend, or co-worker?

Well, you don't want to set the bar too low, but you don't want to set it so high that it becomes overwhelming for you, right? Expect the same from yourself that you would expect from others. Also, learn to forgive yourself and others when, on occasions, you can't meet those standards – it's called being human. Learn to ask for and accept help. Delegate responsibilities to others and let them handle it their way. It's okay to let go, once in a while.

## ORGANIZE YOURSELF

Multi-tasking has become an essential part of life these days. Demanding professional, personal and social commitments can sometimes lead to overwork and fatigue, the most common causes of stress. The solution lies in trying to organize broad time slots for every activity through the day. The timelines may sometimes not be easy to follow but as you learn to organize yourself, things will start falling in place.

It is also essential to understand that sometimes you may be taking on too much. Learn to say 'no' to things that are not really important. Instead, make time for activities and pastimes that make you happy and peaceful. Manage your time well. If you work better in the morning, plan your big tasks for the morning. If you're a night owl, plan your important tasks for later in the day.

## DEVELOP A STRONG EMOTIONAL AND SOCIAL NETWORK

Do you have someone you can talk to about your life? Having someone you can share both the good and bad with is important. If you are not happy with a large group of friends, try and identify a few trustworthy and genuine friends whom you can lean on in times of difficulty. You wouldn't turn them away if they needed you, would you?

If you have particular interests, it works really well to join a group or organization where people share those interests. Sometimes it is rejuvenating to debate and talk about topics that one is passionate about.

If you feel that you need guided assistance in helping cope with any form of stress, do not shy away from seeking assistance from professionals - counsellors, health care experts or healers who are experienced in giving support.

## LET IT OUT, ONCE IN A WHILE

Laugh. Cry. Scream. Sometimes you need to let out your emotions and very few tools are better than the ones nature has given us. But it would be sensible to save these emotional outbursts for a private, comfortable setting.

Having a good cry on the shoulder of a loved one or a good belly laugh with a set of close friends or a loud yell, preferably in the privacy of your car, can prove to be a great stress-buster. These mechanisms offer some of the most immediate means of stress relief. However, remember that they shouldn't be your only way of dealing with stress.

## MINI DOSES

Give yourself loving, positive and affirming messages throughout the day.

Before you go to bed, try and recall any instance during the day that made you happy, even momentarily, and sleep with that thought.

— ❧ —

Practice any form of exercise.

— ❧ —

Try and walk in nature any time of the day.

— ❧ —

Listen to music.

— ❧ —

Dance/ Cook / Sing / Read –
Do whatever makes you happy.

— ❧ —

Try deep breathing or gently tap on your heart centre (at your work desk).

— ❧ —

Seek out warm friends whom you can be
comfortable with, the way you are.

Eat Chocolate, Sip Tea/ Coffee and Relax.

*"Meditation is not a withdrawal from life.
Meditation is a process of understanding oneself"*

— **J Krishnamurti**

# CHAPTER 5
## CALMING THE MIND — MEDITATION

———— ◆◆◆ ————

Now that we have redefined Stress, let me take on another highly misconstrued concept, termed 'MEDITATION'. For most of us who have not practiced any form of it or never experienced its benefits, Meditation seems to be limited to robed gurus or monks high up in the mountains. But you would be surprised to know that modern-day spirituality thinks otherwise. It brands Meditation as one of the most effective ways to cut down stress and anxiety emerging from professional and personal demands. In fact, scientific research shows that the practice has an almost laughably long list of health benefits too, from lowering your blood pressure to boosting your immune system to essentially rewiring your brain for happiness.

If this is the case, why is it that so many of us shy

away from Meditation or fail to even recognize its benefits? It's simply because, much like Spirituality, there is no clarity on what Meditation entails or what one can achieve through it. Adding to the confusion is the fact that there are so many different types of meditative practices -Transcendental Meditation, Vipassana, Zen, Stillness and Devotional Meditation. So is each one different? Let me put it this way. Though each methodology is different, all meditative practices share a lot of common elements. The choice of your meditative practice will depend purely on which form you are able to practice best and benefit most from. None is more effective than the other. Personally, I tried out many forms before finally hitting upon the Chakra Dhyana mediation technique that is simple, less time-consuming and very effective. I will detail it in the later part of the book for those who wish to try it out for themselves. However, I say with surety that it is best to start any meditation practice under a guide or practitioner, so it becomes easier to follow the process.

Before moving ahead, let me now reveal some startling misconceptions about meditation that I have come across during my many discussions and interactions. These misconceptions have not only kept many away from beginning a meditative practice, but also caused unrealistic expectations about what meditation can help you achieve. It is imperative to tide over most of these for realistic results.

## MEDITATION MEANS THINKING ABOUT NOTHING

I hear this almost every day. People say to me, "I can't meditate, because I can't turn off my mind." Well, the human mind is like a clock that ticks 24 hours of the day, 365 days of the year. To demand that the mind stop working and think of nothing is an impossible task. In fact, trying to think of nothing will surely make you think of something.

Meditation is not about thinking of nothing. True meditation is about slowing the mind and being aware of your thoughts. Meditation does not require that you empty your mind. Meditation requires you to be aware of your thoughts and reactions. By focusing on the thinking process, the space between each thought will increase, your thinking will calm down, and you will relax. Meditation will help you make peace with whatever is going on in your mind. Initially there will be a lot of mental chatter but as you keep going with your practice, you will develop the will power to let thoughts come and go, and be a bystander.

## MEDITATION MEANS GOING INTO
## A STATE OF MENTAL STUPOR

Meditation is not about zoning out, achieving unconsciousness, or escaping reality. In fact, meditation is geared toward achieving a greater awareness of ourselves and our thinking process. Meditation is a more direct, raw experience of reality. When you meditate, you learn to acknowledge the internal chatter and focus on the precise emotion you are experiencing, thereby experiencing it with full intensity. Meditation enables you to have the courage to face intense emotions and experience them in all their rawness.

Meditation provides you with the chance to sit with your emotions and actually experience them. This process is initially challenging but, ultimately, you will feel relieved and extremely liberated because the thoughts that you have tried to curtail and shut off will be released. Facing your emotions and acknowledging them will give you mental stamina and emotional resilience, to make decisions that are not influenced by your feelings.

## MEDITATION IS ONLY FOR HOLY PEOPLE

To meditate, you must be enlightened, become a

vegetarian, be religious, and do away with bad thoughts. Right? Wrong! Meditation does not require you to alter personal preferences or choices. It does not require you to give up anything that you like. And it requires no special set-up. Mediation is a practice of calm, focused thinking and attention. It is available to, and effective for, everyone.

Meditation is for people like you and me who work every day and have to make decisions on what to buy or sell; whom to hire or fire, date or marry, think of how to meet a tough deadline or whether to say yes or no to a boring cocktail party. Meditation is for people who face the daily pressures of trying to balance work with healthy family lives and relationships. Meditation is for each one of us.

## MEDITATION TAKES UP TOO MUCH TIME

This turns out to be the most common snag for a majority I meet. In fact, frankly, I also held this notion till the time I practically tried out meditation. Loads of professionals who come for my sessions say, "I already don't have enough time to do all I want, so how can I start a daily practice?" Well, for many of us, time is already in short supply so it seems nearly impossible to make time for a meditative practice. However, the paradox is that meditation actually creates more time for daily activities.

The deep rest you get in meditation actually helps clear your mind so that you become a more effective thinker. In turn, you are able to make decisions faster and therefore have more time in your day. By taking time out to focus the mind, you make decisions in a more considered way. As you grow in your practice, you will also realize that the effective time you spend with your family or at work will increase in intensity and quality.

My meditation teacher assured me that one minute of meditation is equivalent to ten minutes of deep sleep. I recommend that beginners start off with 10-15 minutes of meditation initially; this will be enough to get you started.

## MEDITATION IS ONLY ABOUT RELAXATION

You could think of meditation as practiced relaxation - the process of concentrating the mind, calming the body, and shutting out external stressors. These are key relaxation techniques and are also the first steps in any meditation practice. But meditation is much more than relaxation. It enables you to delve deep inside yourself, into the subconscious and unconscious levels of your mind. Through this, you gain an awareness of what drives your actions and what underlies your decision-making processes. Simply, it means that your decisions come from awareness, not from mental clutter or extreme emotion.

Today, we are all living in an impatient world where we often do things mindlessly... reaching into the fridge when we're not hungry, checking our e-mail or phone messages while we are in conversation with other people, or losing our temper on small little things, only to regret it later. This is where the practice of meditation and its concept of mindfulness helps, by making us respond thoughtfully, rather than react thoughtlessly, to the world around us.

The ability to see what's going on in your head at any given moment without reacting to it blindly is a superpower and believe me, it can be achieved through meditation. Personally, I started with about 10-15 minutes of meditation a day, and very quickly noticed a few benefits: ● Increased focus, ● A greater sense of calm, and ● A vastly improved ability to jolt myself out of rumination about the past or future, back to whatever was happening right in front of my face. Today, my personal and professional life is much richer, all thanks to my meditative practice.

I am certainly not arguing that meditation is a panacea. But through experience I have realized that my Chakra Dhyana meditation technique has definitely made me happier, calmer, and extremely tolerant. I have found that meditation has helped me strike a perfect balance between striving and stress, between ambition and inner peace.

*"If you worry about what might be, and wonder what might have been, you will ignore what is."*

— **Unknown**

# CHAPTER 6
## LIVING IN NOW

L et me start this chapter by asking you a simple question. Take a minute off and answer. What is the one action, the one thought, the one moment of TODAY that you are most thankful for?

Most of us might probably take a long time to think and ponder over the answer. It's because between all our chaotic, mundane activities, we barely stop to think about 'TODAY', about 'NOW'. We forget to appreciate the living present because our "monkey minds" as Buddhists call them, vault from thought to thought, like monkeys swinging from tree to tree. When work stress builds up, we yearn for a vacation. But once on vacation, our mind shuttles back, and most of us keep worrying about the work piling up back at office. We incessantly keep checking on our mails and messages.

Even the world around us contributes in a major way to mental fragmentation, disintegration and incoherence. We have got accustomed to 'doing' things almost mindlessly, every day.

Most of us are highly stressed-out over work or relationship issues, worrying about things that could potentially happen or over-planning for the future, completely missing out on the present. In fact a whole lot of us stress about things that have already happened, that are unchangeable because they are in the past. We dwell on intrusive memories of the past or fret about what may or may not happen in the future. Between all this, there is not a moment of stillness and calm.

Our lives are so much more wonderful than we give them credit for. If we were to individually sit and reflect, we have a million things to thank the universe for. But surprisingly, life doesn't seem so wonderful, after all. Well, it's mostly because very few of us are living in it... we are stuck in another time zone. It may sound strange but there always seems as though there is something in the past we keep thinking about... or something in the distant future that we keep looking forward to, which never lets us focus in the present moment.

Think about it, how often are you worrying about things that have yet to come? How often do you keep beating yourself up for mistakes that you've made, no matter how long ago? All this contributes to unwanted mental stress that can have a detrimental effect on your health.

This is where developing the skill of 'LIVING IN NOW' can help. Living in the present can have a dramatic effect on your emotional and physical well-being.

When you learn to live in the present, you learn to accept. You accept life as it is now, not as how you wish it would have been or how it might be. You learn to forgive yourself for the mistakes you've made, because you realize that nothing from the past can ever change and there is no point stressing over it.

You learn to face life challenges more systematically and strategically. You take planned decisions that are not ruled by the fear of the future or negative happenings from the past. When you're living in now, in acceptance, you realize everything is complete as it is.

Living a consistently mindful life takes effort. But mindfulness itself is easy. Here is a very simple exercise that will help you understand what 'Mindfulness' practically means. 'Mindfulness' is the only intentional, systematic activity that is not about trying to improve yourself or to get anywhere. It is simply a matter of realizing where you already are. Remember, at the end of this exercise…'Nothing happens Next'.

You do not need to decide a time and venue for this exercise. You can become mindful at any moment, just by paying attention to your immediate experience. You can do it right now.

Start thinking of what's happening this instant? Just observe the moment. What do you see, hear, sense, smell? Whether good or bad, pleasant or unpleasant—be in the moment. Do not judge it. If you notice your mind wandering, bring yourself back. Just say to yourself, "Now. Now. Now." Try this exercise a few times every day and see how you become more observant and aware of things happening to you or around you. You start seeing things from a fresh perspective, breaking the monotony of everyday rhythms. You start effectively understanding the feeling of 'Living in Now'.

Since I am on the topic, let me give you the practical lowdown on what you can do to start living life in the present.

## DO AWAY WITH UNNEEDED POSSESSIONS

Remove objects and items that you associate with negative memories of the past. Minimalism forces you to live in the present and helps you to stop living in the past.

## FORGIVE AND FORGET

If you are harboring resentment towards anyone because of past hurts, choose to forgive, not for them but for yourself. Learn to move on. The harm caused might be their fault. But allowing it to impact you is purely yours.

## STOP WORRYING

As bad as it is worrying about the past, it's equally bad worrying about the future. Realize that tomorrow is going to happen whether you worry about it or not. And since worry has never accomplished anything for anyone, redirect your mental energy towards affirmative action for a safe and bright future. Let worry take up no mental space.

## DREAM BIG, BUT DON'T LET DREAMS TAKE OVER HARD WORK

Set goals and plans for the future. But start doing the base work today. Don't allow dreaming about tomorrow replace hard work today.

## FIND OUT WHAT YOU LOVE ABOUT YOUR JOB

If you just about 'survive' the workweek, constantly waiting for the weekend, you are wasting a major part of your life. The best solution would be to find a new job that you actually enjoy, but here's a more practical piece of advice. Find something that you appreciate about your current job or profile that is keeping you on. Focus on that rather than the negatives.

## THINK OUT OF THE BOX FOR SOLUTIONS TO EVERYDAY PROBLEMS

You might be stuck to the cliché 'That's how we have always done it' but believe me, yesterday's solutions don't work well in today's environment. Try telling your child not to play on the iPad because your parents never allowed you to. But were iPads so prevalent when you were kids? Well, our world is changing so fast that most of yesterday's solutions are no longer the right answers today. Work out a solution aimed at today, for today.

## GET OVER ADDICTIONS

When I talk of addictions, I do not mean only

cigarettes or drinks. I am also talking of simple little addictions that we get hooked on to every day, like the latest addiction of checking on our whatsapp messages 24 hours of the day, even when our kid is trying to discuss an important happening at school. Addictions start holding you hostage. They restrict your mind from having any free space. Start doing away with these addictions. Let them be around but remove their influence over your life.

## FULLY APPRECIATE EACH MOMENT

It is essential to soak in as much of today as you possibly can. Observe and enjoy each sight, each sound, each smell. Feel every emotion - triumph, happiness, anger and sorrow. Do not let any emotion go unnoticed.

## THINK OF WHAT YOU ACCOMPLISH
## EACH DAY. THANK THE UNIVERSE

If you are still thinking about what you did yesterday or what you will do tomorrow, you haven't done much today. At the end of each day, list out on paper or in your mind, the accomplishments of the day – big or small. Think of what good happened to you or what good you did.

Do not forget to thank the universe for whatever little good happened today.

## SMILE

I say this in the end so each of you surely remembers. Begin each day with a big smile. You are in control of your attitude every morning - keep it optimistic and expectant. Smile through the day, at whatever instance possible. It changes the atmosphere.

Most importantly, find a sense of balance. Once in a while, switch off, pause, and let your mind be still. Stop 'doing' and focus on just 'being'. If you choose to actively live in the present, you can appreciate life for all that it is...HERE and NOW. In the present there are no regrets and no anxiety. Life just is...

*'Be Thankful, Be Peaceful, Be Happy'*

# CHAPTER 7
## THE HIGH ROAD TO HAPPINESS

Tell me frankly; is it not a pleasure to meet people who are always smiling and happy? They always seem high on life, energetic and enthusiastic. They emit an exuberance of joy that is almost contagious. You scratch your head because from the outside, they don't seem to have any more than you do and their problems seem just as big. Then why is it that they can find a hundred reasons to smile while you can't? Well, these are probably people who have hit the high road to Happiness – learning to be Peaceful, Contented and Thankful.

Most of us have been raised with extremely erroneous notions about Happiness. We tend to believe that the more we have, the happier we will be. So much so that a whole lot of us dedicate our lives pursuing the wrong ideals. We end up thinking career success guarantees happiness, or an accomplishment or achievement will make us happy, or that happiness will come from making superficial changes in lifestyles and living standards. In fact, if you ask me, none of these can or will ensure Happiness. Each success or accomplishment will quickly make you excited and happy but the joyous reaction will be short-lived. After some time, you will fall back into your regular cycle of work, responsibility, stress, desire, and anxiety.

So is there really a technique that one can practice to be Happy always? Unbelievably, there is. But whether you want to make your life happier is a matter of pure choice. You can choose to be sad when everything is going well and you can choose to be happy even when nothing seems right.

However, before mastering the art of staying Happy, it is essential to understand that Happiness is an internal state of being, not an external phenomenon. Nothing in the world can make you happy if there is no internal urge. Your mindset, your thought process and your perception of Happiness itself will determine how happy or unhappy you will be through life. To be happy at all times, you need to make happiness a habit and not just an act.

Happiness is hard to define but each of us is clearly aware of whether we are happy or not. For most people, happiness seems to be the outcome of positive events. It is usually driven by a win, gain, or achievement. It is likely that these external events trigger a happy state but this kind of happiness is fleeting and temporary. The state of true happiness actually comes from the inside, and no external circumstance or situation can affect it. True happiness comes from 'Total Freedom' – freedom from emotions, expectations and opinions.

I have had cases where people have walked up to me and said extremely illogical stuff like 'Happiness is a form of luck. Some people are destined to be happy while others like me are destined to be unhappy always.' I completely disagree. If you want to be happy, you need to understand that you can be happy and that you should be happy. We can all lead positively great lives provided we make up our mind to not let any thought or situation get powerful enough to pull us down and keep us unhappy for long. Each of us is equipped with the power to bounce back after a pull-down provided we harness the strength of positive thinking.

Many people also make the mistake of believing that they don't deserve happiness, and accept their unhappy state as their destiny. The truth of the matter is that happiness, like anything else in life, needs to be nurtured.

Ask yourself what makes you happy, and find ways to restructure your life so that you are able to do more of those things. Everyone has unique requirements for attaining happiness and what makes one person happy may be very different from what makes the other happy. Revel in your individuality and do not worry about whether or not your desires are comparable to those of your peers.

## DEALING WITH 'UNHAPPINESS'

All of us go through ups and downs in life; there are positive and negative events and occurrences. Some life events certainly do not evoke happy reactions. But the secret to Happiness lies in not letting any situation or event overpower your mental positivity and influence long-term relationships and feelings. Temporary low troughs and mood swings are totally human and okay as long as they do not negatively affect your perspective of life, of yourself and people around you.

Let me try and suggest some practical tips on what you can do to rid yourself of Unhappiness.

## FIND A SOLUTION

When something goes wrong, try to figure out a solution instead of wallowing in self-pity. Do not keep thinking about the problem itself or reliving a situation or event. That will definitely make you unhappy. It is essential that you take appropriate action, keeping in mind a solution-driven approach. If the solution lies in reconciling with a situation you cannot change, try and find positives, especially at your workplace. Truly happy people do not allow setbacks to affect their mood, because they know that with a little thought they can turn the circumstances back to their favor. In an unhappy situation, try and change your perspective. No situation or event can last forever. Work out a solution and get it out of your head. Let nothing bother you forever.

If your unhappiness comes from an individual, take time in analyzing whether this individual is important enough to put you completely off track or if there is some way of letting go of this person or cutting them out from your life completely. In professional circles, it is best to minimize your interactions with people who make you unhappy or troubled.

If personal relationships are causing you grief, it is best to open up and talk about what is bothering you or making you unhappy. Problems and situations get complicated if solutions are not worked out quickly. Also remember that while working out solutions, the mental frame has to be open and positive and not ridden by past thoughts or actions of the individual. Do not be too judgemental or harsh while taking personal decisions. It is best to be wise, accommodating and considerate while finding solutions to personal issues. Remember, these solutions are crucial for ensuring internal peace and happiness.

## COUNT YOUR ACCOMPLISHMENTS
## FOR THE DAY

Usually, we begin each day with the desire to accomplish several objectives. Often, even if we accomplish a lot during the day, we feel frustrated because of some minor tasks we did not accomplish. Even after spending the entire day successfully carrying out plans, instead of feeling happy and satisfied we start feeling unhappy looking at what was not accomplished.

The solution lies in looking at what you have done and not at what you have not been able to do. Do not keep putting off your plans, but if you have not been able to finish what you started for the day, complete it as soon as you get the time and space. Before you go to bed, don't forget to count your accomplishments for the day, big or small.

## CHANGE THE WAY YOU LOOK AT THINGS

Endeavour to change the way you look at things. Believe me; this practice will take the longest to perfect. Always look at the bright side. The mind might drag you to think about negativity and difficulties. Start directing the mind to look at good and positive aspects of every life situation. Watch your thoughts. Whenever you catch yourself thinking negative, start thinking of pleasant and good things that have happened to you since childhood. Your thoughts will slowly change to the positive.

## STAY DETACHED

When things do not proceed as intended and desired, and you do need to face an unhappy event or situation, stay detached. Do not attach more meaning and importance to an event or occurrence than required. Think about it; when most of us are put in tough situations, instead of working out solutions, we often start asking unwanted questions like 'Why does it have to happen to me? Why is God punishing me? Why do I have this kind of fate? Why did I need to get into this situation?' This 'Why Me' attitude is in fact one of the biggest culprits leading to unhappiness. It is important that whenever you face a tough situation, take a detached look at the problem. Try and work out a solution as if you were finding it for a loved one and not yourself. Look at the problem from an outsider's perspective and then work out a solution. Detachment will help you stay calm, control your reactions and help you take intelligent decisions.

## EACH DAY, DO SOMETHING TO MAKE YOURSELF AND OTHERS HAPPY

Doing something big is not necessarily an indicator of how 'Happy' you will be. Very small gestures and acts every day can make you and others happy.

For a start, when you step out of bed, set off with a nice big Smile. Try and greet everyone you meet. Pass on a kind word or a gentle appreciative remark to people around. Help your colleagues, stop your car at the crossroad to let people cross, or just get home a small surprise gift or pretty flowers for someone you love. The possibilities are infinite.

Do not forget to do something nice for yourself as

well. Grab a bite of your favourite chocolate, read a book, watch a nice TV show or just spend some fun time with your little one. All these things will not only bring down the unhappiness quotient for the day but make you quiet, peaceful and happy as you go to bed.

*"Gratitude can transform common days into thanks givings, turn routine jobs into joy, and change ordinary opportunities into blessings."*

— **William Arthur Ward**

# CHAPTER 8
## GRATITUDE — THANK YOUR BEING

———————◆◆◆———————

Talking of Happiness, let me move on to another crucial factor that will strongly determine your Happiness quotient in life – GRATITUDE. By definition, Gratitude is the quality of being thankful with a readiness to show appreciation for kindness and being kind in return. But it is important to understand that practical application of the Gratitude formula can greatly enhance Happiness and peace in your life.

This might sound a little farfetched, especially to the skeptics, but studies prove that deliberately cultivating a sense of gratitude can make your mind more peaceful, and increase well-being and happiness. People who regularly practise gratitude, by taking time to notice and reflect upon the things they are thankful for, experience more positive emotions, feel more alive, sleep better, express more compassion and kindness, and even have stronger immune systems.

With so many hidden benefits, why is it that most of us fail to practise Gratitude? The problem is, most of us aren't hardwired to be grateful. Loads of people that I talk to, do understand the dictionary meaning of the word very well, but barely understand what 'Gratitude' means in practical terms. Many feel slightly silly about the exercise of activating their gratitude. Others find it tough to find reasons and things to be grateful or thankful for. Let me tell you out of experience that Gratitude is one trait that does not come naturally to most of us. I was as lost when I started on my understanding of Thankfulness. Today I can surely say that like any life skill, gratitude will require patient practice but it is a skill worth acquiring.

The process of exploring Gratitude will be a simple one, but you will have to pass through various stages on your Gratitude graph to understand its practical application.

**Stage 1:** The first stage, which is the toughest, will be to **start recognizing what you are grateful for.**

By force of habit, most of us take things for granted. We think that everything that happens in life, at least most of the mundane things – good or bad, happen of their own volition. It is only in extraordinary turnarounds that we start paying gratitude to the Universe. It is a sad fact that barely any of us feel the need to express gratitude towards anything in our routine, everyday lives.

Just for a few moments, consider the things you have in your life that you could be grateful for. All your relationships, material comforts, your body, and a mind that allows you to understand yourself and everything around you. The mere ability to breathe freely, the air that is filling your lungs and making life possible, you need to be thankful for each of these things, every day. But how many of us even acknowledge this fact? Exploring Gratitude will make you aware and thankful for the small little blessings that we so often ignore.

Paying attention to life's positives will train you to see more and more of them, which will help you become more grateful. You will feel blessed that good weather allowed you to get out for a nice morning jog, that you made it to the bus on time, or that your kids offered to help wind up the kitchen. Life's little instances will give you reason to be thankful.

A conscious focus on gratitude will also remind you of unobtrusive pluses that get lost in the ups and downs of a busy life - the most important ones being a family, health and home. Grateful reflection will help you pick out and savour every little good that is happening in life. Slowly, your mind will divert itself to looking at the positives rather than focus on the negatives, in every life situation. This power of positive thinking will give you the strength to remain stable and peaceful, both in routine and unexpected situations.

But the process of Thankfulness or Gratitude will take time to activate. Initially you might find it strange or silly to keep looking out for things to be thankful for and thanking the universe for all that is around. So, till Gratitude comes naturally to you, my mantra will be to 'Fake it'. Yes, I truly mean it. Initially you will have to artificially push yourself to thank the universe for things around and keep saying 'Thank you' in the most unnatural way. But once you activate this process, your mind will start falling in line with your words. You will start to look at life's positives in the most natural way and slowly start identifying a million things worth being thankful for.

**Stage 2:** The second stage would involve **acknowledging the small little things that make a difference to everyday life** and thanking the universe for them. Since mental training will take some time, the best and easiest way would be to start jotting your Thankfulness down on paper, in words. Simply keep a gratitude journal, regularly writing brief reflections on moments for which you are thankful, each day. Gratitude needn't be reserved only for momentous occasions like a promotion at work or an expensive gift from your loved one. You can also be thankful for something as simple as a delicious meal or a small outing to the neighbourhood park.

This exercise will give you a short-term mood boost. Once you get started, you will slowly find more and more things to jot down and be grateful for. Your happiness will last all year round.

**Stage 3:** The third and final stage would require maximum effort to tide over and be practised... **thanking the universe for what you have instead of what you don't.**

The mind is a mischievous player. It always works around 'what is not', rather than 'what is'. This is one of the biggest reasons why most of us never realize gratitude. Because we spend a whole lot of mental energy focused on what we don't have. The negatives always overshadow the positives.

Whether we agree or disagree, whether we are aware of it or not, the Universe supports us in many ways. But more than often, we take for granted the things that have gone right in our lives. Our natural tendency is to focus on perceived problems that we encounter daily.

There is no doubt that this tendency is necessary to advance in personal relationships and our careers. It is this tendency that pushes us to achieve more and progress ahead.

But it is crucial to bear in mind that ambition and aspiration should not take away thankfulness for the moment, for what life is offering right now, today. Sometimes we need to pause and reflect on our bounty. We need to thank the Universe for what we have, not only in terms of material comforts but unseen blessings in the form of family, a home and relationships – personal and professional. The feeling of gratitude will keep us rooted and help us look at positives even in tough situations.

Let me also truthfully say that it is easy to be grateful when things are going well. It can be more difficult during the trials of life: death, disease, rejection, or failure. Often in a stuck moment, it's hard to see positive forces, when obstacles are glaring and fears are looming. The truth is that no one is exempt from the trials of life, but good can always be found even in the worst of times. Embracing gratitude during trial periods will help you get through any life situation without getting badly shaken. Gratitude will help lessen panic, and open up your thinking to new solutions.

Practically, let me explain how Gratitude works best in tough times. Think of the worst times in your life, your sorrows, your losses, your sadness—and then observe the situation you are in today, right now. Remember that you made it through the worst times of your life, you got through the trauma, you got through the trial, you endured the temptation, you survived bad relationships and you still have a lot around you. This is what you can be thankful for the strength to have sailed through hard times. Gratitude helps put situations into perspective. When you are able to see the good through the bad, you have fewer reasons to complain. In the long run, Gratefulness will make you stronger and more resilient, and slowly build up mental strength that is so required during tough times.

Once you begin to practise Gratitude, you will realise and observe the changes that will happen in your reactions, your mindset and also in your physical state of being. Your dissatisfaction levels will reduce drastically, you will gain a general sense of contentment, and you will become less judgemental, as a result of which you will feel better not only about others but also about yourself. You will feel more energetic and alert, exercise more and sleep better. Gratitude will neutralize stress and contribute to overall health.

As a starter, let me give you a few suggestions on how you can start cultivating Gratitude in everyday being. If you expect results, it will be fine to begin each of these exercises with scepticism, but not with cynicism.

Keep a gratitude journal. All it requires is noting one or more things you are grateful for on a daily basis. No fancy notebook, no computer program required.

⁓⁓⁓

If you identify something negative, switch your mind to thinking of something positive. If you identify someone with a negative trait, instead of exaggerating the thought, think about some positive trait of that person and shift focus to it. Don't try and stop negative thoughts but counter them with positive ones.

⁓⁓⁓

When you find yourself in a bad situation, ask: What can I learn from here, when I look back on this situation, without emotion?

⁓⁓⁓

Try not to complain or criticize, unless it works for some good. Notice the amount of energy you are wasting on these unwanted actions.

⁓⁓⁓

Give at least one compliment daily. It can be in appreciation to a person or to nature around.

Take a quiet gratitude walk. This can be anywhere, in your neighbourhood, inside your house or simply around your office. Though ideally anywhere in the open would be better. As you walk, consider the many things which you are grateful for - loving relationships, material comforts, the body that allows you to experience the world, and the mind that allows you to really understand things. Pay attention to your senses—everything you're seeing, hearing, feeling, smelling, and maybe even tasting—and see how many things you can find to feel grateful for.

Stop sometime of the day and thank someone. Make an unexpected phone call to say thank you for something that someone assisted you with during the day, whether it is your helper, your co-worker, friends or family. You will change your day and theirs, by a simple Thank You, expressing your gratitude for their small little act.

Write tiny 'Thank You' notes. While we may often thank people verbally, the written word can be even more powerful because someone has taken the time to write their appreciation.
You can get into the habit of posting small thank-you notes. These can also be re-read and treasured, creating joy and love that will continue to ripple out into the universe.

⁂

Become involved in a cause that is important to you. Donate money, time or talent. By joining in, you will gain greater appreciation for the organization, and it will appreciate you more, too.

⁂

Each day, as you wake up in the morning or before you go to bed, take time to remember and reclaim what is so amazingly good in your life. Gratitude means saying "Yes" to the life you've been given. Accept the good gifts of life that are actually there, free of resentment for what is not there, and away from the yearning for more. Complete the daily chapters of your life by remembering and appreciating what has been so very good till now, till today…

⁂

*True Forgiveness is not an action; it is an attitude.*

# CHAPTER 9
## FORGIVENESS

———————◆◆◆———————

After Gratitude, let me guide you through another potent practice that can make life a lot more pleasant, a lot more enjoyable and highly uncomplicated - 'Forgiveness'.

We need to understand that holding onto anger hurts us more than it hurts the object of that anger. Unresolved anger can create health problems just as unmanaged stress can, and it robs us of happiness as well. Knowing this, however, doesn't always make the anger magically dissolve. We need to get it out of our system. The best way of doing this is by finding a practical solution and implementing a plan to rid ourselves of the anger and irritation. But in many instances, even after working out a realistic solution, a lot of bitterness and grudge still remains. This is exactly where

Forgiveness steps in. Forgiveness practically frees your mind from struggling and striving. Forgiveness sets you free. It helps you do away with negative emotions that the mind attaches to people, incidents or episodes.

In fact, a study from the *Journal of Behavioural Medicine* says that apart from psychological benefits, the practice of Forgiveness has major physical benefits too. The study suggests that practising Forgiveness lowers heart rate and blood pressure and works well to relieve stress. It is literally good for your heart. Practising Forgiveness also improves your sleep quality and rids you of fatigue and somatic complaints. Forgiveness not only restores positive thoughts, feelings and behaviour towards who the mind terms as the 'offending party', but this positivity also spills over into behaviours towards all relationships – personal and professional.

But despite all its benefits, practically pursuing Forgiveness can be a real challenge. In most situations, it is extremely difficult to forgive. Why? Let me first start by detailing a few misconceptions that stop most of us from practicing this powerful trait. Let's analyze what we usually read of Forgiveness.

## WE THINK FORGIVENESS MEANS
## APPROVAL

More often than not, we mistake forgiving the 'other' person as saying what they did was okay, or that they are welcome to do it again. Neither of these is true. Forgiving does not mean that you do not condemn the action of the other person, but it means that you let go of the latent anger that keeps brewing inside you as a result of that action. Understand that this persistent state of bitterness hurts you and affects your relationships – connected and unconnected.

Incidents and episodes are usually circumstance-driven, so realize that whatever action or reaction took place at a certain time was momentary and probably involuntary. It would be sensible and wise to 'pardon or let go'. Whatever the argument, the most crucial tenet here is that 'You forgive for yourself and not for anyone else'. Forgiveness needs to be practised for your stability, peace of mind and wellness. If you do not forgive, then a part of your inner energy is trapped in resentment, anger, pain, or suffering of some kind. This trapped energy slows you down, frustrates you and makes it difficult for you to look beyond. As you learn to forgive, the energy which was going into unhappy thoughts and feelings gets liberated and flows into creating positivity inside and around you rather than adding to mental and physical suffering. But do remember, while it is essential for you to forgive, it is equally vital to take steps towards protecting yourself from being hurt in the future.

## WE THINK THAT THE OTHER PERSON DOES NOT DESERVE BEING FORGIVEN

Whenever I speak to someone about Forgiving, the first response I get is 'They do not deserve to be forgiven for what they did'. Forgiveness can be difficult because it feels like we are letting those who have wronged us 'off the hook'. We feel that the person doesn't deserve our forgiveness. At such points, remember that forgiveness benefits the forgiver more than the one who is forgiven.

Even if the other person does not deserve our forgiveness, we do deserve to be free of the anger that hurts us. More often than not, the anger that you hold towards someone keeps you miserable but the 'offending party' might not even be affected. In the true sense, you need to forgive for your own self and your peace of mind, and less for the other person.

Whenever the mind blocks you from forgiving, ask yourself this important question, is the entire episode or incident worth wasting energy on? If you can change the situation in any way or bring about a change in the person who has hurt you, keep trying; but when that is not the case, take the incident as just another happening in life and move on. Arm yourself with a clear understanding that it's not worth the effort.

## WE KEEP FEELING THAT THE PAIN IS STILL FRESH

Whenever we think about forgiving the person who has offended us, we are reminded of what they did, and we become angry all over again. We keep reliving the episode and amplify our pain and trauma. There is no doubt that it is hard to let go of what has hurt you so much. It is tough to forgive someone who has committed unacceptable behaviour.

But it is equally important to accept that whatever happened was in the past. The episode or incident is already over and life has moved on. Reliving the scenario will only add to your mental agony. You will have to work on accepting that what happened is over. Again remember, you are accepting the situation for your own sake, not for anyone else's.

By refusing to forgive others, you will keep making yourself unhappy. Forgiveness will free up your mental and emotional energies so that you can apply them to create a better life for yourself and focus on your goals, not on insignificant incidents and episodes. You will set yourself free from the past. Your thinking will be clearer and more positive. You will have an open and optimistic attitude to people in your life and they will respond more positively to you in return.

Remember; when you forgive, you become a happier person. You are able to focus your energies on what you need to achieve or what you can share with others. When you forgive you are more open to success because rather than mindless anger, you work towards whatever is meaningful to you. As you learn to forgive, what seemed impossible becomes possible.

Practically speaking, Forgiveness is one trait that will have to be cultivated slowly every single day. But as a starter, you can assign one day when you sit and think consciously about all that has hurt you and is still bothering you every day. Having been through a whole lot of healing sessions, I realize that most of us have a lot of bitterness and anger about people and incidents that we keep suppressing constantly. It is only when there are outbursts that all this anger spills out. We barely even try and bring to the surface these buried feelings and think about letting go. We pull along every day, carrying this unwanted burden of negativity. So here's what you can practically do.

**Step I** - Begin with one day in a week when you design your own **'Forgiveness day'.**

- ✯ Take time to consciously think about anyone you may be angry with, for whatever reason, even if that anger is not fresh. Then as consciously, decide to let go.
- ✯ If there is a lot to forgive, just let go of as much as you can for now, and work on it again later.
- ✯ Forgive your parents if you are holding onto anger from your childhood.
- ✯ Forgive people you grew up with if you had some childhood experiences you're still angry about.
- ✯ Forgive your spouse or partner if you have any relationship baggage that you're holding onto. If it feels difficult to forgive because you're afraid that you'll open yourself up to getting hurt by them again, realize that the anger itself is hurting you, but you can take steps to change your relationship and the way you are treated in it.
- ✯ Forgive your co-workers for how they treat you or what politics they play with you. Focus on the positive points that you possess, which forces them to behave in a particular manner, and forgive.

✻ Forgive yourself if you're feeling any self-directed anger for anything, such as goals you haven't met, promises to yourself you haven't fulfilled, or mistakes you've made in the past. Just let it all go!

**Step II** - Even after you decide to let go of your anger and forgive, you will be stumped by the question **'How to Forgive?'** While everyone may have a unique perspective on how to forgive, there are a few strategies that practically work well.

## EXPRESS YOURSELF

The first and best way is to express your disturbing feelings. In certain instances, it may not help to express your feelings to the other person. If the person is not important, and you find it ok, gently cut off the relationship. But if a relationship is important to you and you would like to maintain it, do tell the other person, in non-threatening language, how their actions affected you.

If you feel that things will get much worse if you address the situation directly, talk to someone trusted, and ease your pain. Another strategy that works well is to write down all that you feel inside on a piece of paper and tear it up or burn it. This way you will feel less burdened by the emotions pent up inside and it will be a little easier to let go. Throughout the process, you needn't convey to the other person that you are trying to forgive them. The strategy is to get all negative feelings and emotions out of your system and close the chapter in your mind.

## CULTIVATE EMPATHY

I would be lying if I say that it is easy to be empathetic towards someone who has hurt you. But when working on how to forgive, it is essential that you consciously put yourself in the other person's shoes so you might get some understanding on why he/she did what they did. While you do not have to find justification for their actions or agree with what the other person did, empathy can make the process of Forgiveness easier. Instead of simply branding them as 'the enemy,' try to understand the factors that they were dealing with. Maybe they were going through a particularly difficult time in their lives, maybe it was just a sudden, stark reaction, maybe there was more on their mind. Once you assume that their motives were not to purposely cause you pain (unless you have clear indicators otherwise), you may find it easier to forgive. It would also help if you can try and acknowledge some good qualities of the 'other' person that you might be wilfully blinding yourself to.

## PROTECT YOURSELF AND MOVE ON
—❧❧❧—

Apart from forgiving the so called 'anti party', another vital part of the forgiveness process is to work on self-protective plans for the future. It would be intelligent to take every incident or episode as a learning curve and try and gather an understanding of situations. This can be particularly helpful in professional surroundings. If you have a co-worker who continually steals ideas, belittles you or gossips about you, pardon and forgive but ensure that you address the problem by having open discussions with him/her or other concerned authorities. You don't need to hold a grudge in order to protect yourself. Make a plan to address hurtful behaviour, whether in the personal or professional space. But do not let the anger and bitterness stop you from practical thinking and focussed action.

## GET PROFESSIONAL HELP IF YOU NEED IT
—❧❧❧—

Sometimes it can be difficult to forget about the

past and forgive, particularly if the offending acts are ongoing or traumatic. If you're still having difficulty knowing how to forgive someone who's wronged you in a significant way, you may have better success with a therapist who can help you work through your feelings on a deeper level and personally support you through the process.

When you've been deeply hurt, figuring out how to forgive can be difficult. Do not shy away from looking for professional help and guidance in letting go and releasing the stress of the past.

If all this sounds like exaggeration, then let that be for now. Simply practice Forgiveness and observe how the quality of life and relationships change. Learning to forgive will perk up all your relationships, because your attitude to life will improve. Once you learn the skill of forgiving, every aspect of your life will change for the better; at home, at work and in your social circle.

*"For every choice we make, we set a cycle of energy and consequence into motion."*

— **Caroline Myss**

CHAPTER 10
THE ENERGY CYCLE

———————◆◆◆———————

Through all that we have been talking about and focusing on till now, one thing is clear, that your emotional and mental state is as vital as your physical well being, and cannot be ignored in the big scheme of overall health. Addressing your stress and releasing emotional baggage are as crucial for a healthy lifestyle as good sleep, exercise and proper eating.

Believe it or not, your thoughts and emotions, many of which are driven by subconscious beliefs and long-forgotten experiences, are a powerful force that can aid or harm your health. More often than not, mental agony and physical pain are caused by trapped emotions, or trapped energies. Changing how you relate to past experiences, and your emotions, can have a direct impact on your physical health. Once you realize that emotional baggage can adversely affect your health and quality of life, it will become easier to understand how effective, strategies like Energy healing can prove to be.

Since we have hit the topic, let me detail this fascinating aspect of the Mind-Body-Soul connect which I have been extremely fortunate to explore in depth during my many years of spiritual practice – **'The Universal Energy Cycle'**. Quantum physics has proved that almost everything at the sub-atomic level is pure energy. Everything in the universe is made up of energy, including our own bodies. At a universal level, humans and the cosmos are interconnected by an all-pervasive sea of energy that undergirds all phenomena.

The human body itself is a conglomerate of densely packed energy cells. Each cell is broken down into molecules, made up of atoms with protons, neutrons and electrons. These atoms, made of sub-atomic particles, are pure energy. Hence it would not be an exaggeration to say that each of our bodies is one big mass of energy.

Since our body is filled up with energy cells, the root cause of disease is really inharmonious activity at the energetic, sub-atomic level. When you feel an emotion, what you're really sensing is the vibration of a particular energy. Interestingly, each emotion has its own vibratory signature, and when intense emotions are felt, they can become trapped in your body, much like a big ball of energy.

These "energy balls" can get lodged just about anywhere in the body, causing disruptions in the body's energy flow, which underlies the physical system like an invisible matrix. In fact, it is interesting to note that certain emotions can give rise to a sense of discomfort in certain regions of the body. I have had many people suffering from depression complain of chest pain, even though their heart is in perfect condition. When under stress, people often start complaining of stomach aches and digestive upsets. It is important to understand that your energy flow carries thoughts, ideas and emotions to every cell of your body. So a bright and balanced flow of energy is crucial for well-being. Vitalizing and rejuvenating your energy is essential, not only for your emotional balance but for your physical health as well.

The body is a storehouse of memory. Our cells respond to every thought we think and every word we say. Our feelings also affect the electromagnetic field that surrounds us. In fact, each feeling radiates certain vibrations. Positive thoughts create light airy vibrations, while negative thoughts create heavy and dense vibrations. Continuous modes of negative thinking and speaking produce body behaviours that can aggravate physical discomfort. Holding on to negative emotions also upsets the chemical balance in the body. Stress is another major factor that produces significant amounts of chaos at the underlying energetic level. According to reports by The American Medical Association, almost 80 percent of all health problems are stress-related or appear to have an emotional element.

When you are chronically stressed, feelings like anger, aggression, hatred, fear, prejudice, anxiety, insecurity and hopelessness feed the energetic chaos and disrupt the body's natural energy flow. This emotional turmoil manifests as physical pain and disease.

When feelings and emotions are positively transformed, the energy centers in our body vibrate freely and help create trusting relationships, improving effectiveness in high-pressure situations. When we shift out of the negative mode, we activate certain strands of our electrical circuitry. There is a dynamic energy shift in our physical and emotional bodies. The positive vibrations also magnetize positive experiences and change behavioural patterns towards the self and others.

It might sound surprising but clinical trials have confirmed that balancing the body's energy centres rapidly reduces the emotional impact of memories and incidents that trigger emotional distress. Once the distress is reduced or removed, the body can often rebalance itself and heal better.

Energy has to move. If an emotion isn't expressed, it is suppressed. The result of controlling or stifling emotional energy is frustration, anger, depression or physical pain. If emotions are suppressed, self-judgment, low self-esteem and unworthiness begin to develop. This inhibits your ability to create or receive what you really want in life.

Garnering positive thoughts, feelings and emotions are an important aspect of health. They are the tools that can create better lives for each one of us. It is important that we learn to master our emotions so energies in our body flow freely. In my next chapter, I will deal with the practical application of one of the most powerful energy healing techniques that focuses on balancing energy centres or 'Chakras' in the body - **The Chakra Dhyana technique.** This unique practice has worked successfully through time immemorial, helping people heal naturally and effortlessly.

*"Look inwards, create your own reality,
trust your energies and the body will heal itself."*

# CHAPTER 11
## THE INTERPLAY OF ENERGIES
## — BODY CHAKRAS

———— ✦✦✦ ————

Have you ever given any of this a thought? Since creation, the Earth and all other planets have been moving along their orbits, never rolling off from their paths, even for a single moment. A tiny seed has the capacity to hold within it the roots of a gigantic tree. A beautiful child is formed by the mere unison of an egg and a sperm. Some strange life force keeps all of us alive and kicking till our last breath. Most of these phenomena undoubtedly prove that there is some sort of latent energy that is driving the processes of this vast universe.

Quantum physics has proved that everything in this Universe is composed of energy fields, and all things are interconnected. The energy that composes your body is the same as the energy that composes your doors and windows, your computer, your cell phone, animals and trees. This energy is constantly at flow, changing form all the time.

In fact, in sub-atomic physics, elemental reality is conceived, not as "things" but as foci of energy. Specific energy fields, manifesting through individual frequencies, assume distinct forms. This is also true in case of our own bodies. Our personal energy convergence points are a center of reception and radiation. Just as we have a physical anatomy, we have also have an "energy anatomy". Our energy ecosystem is known as the **CHAKRAS**. Chakras are **focused vortices of high, expansive energy, within multiple locations in the body**. There are **7 main Chakras** spanning from the base of the spine to the crown of the head. Connected to these Chakras are **Nadis,** considered to be the vessels through which energy flows. When we move through the day, as we breathe, function, think or even when we are resting, electrical energy is flowing through our bodies via our neurons and nerve pathways.

Biologically, the positions of the major chakras correspond to the major 'nerve plexus' or 'nerve bundles' in our body. These '**nerve bundles'** are associated with major glands. Glands secrete hormones which are critical in the body's chemistry.

Our hormones as well as nerves carry messages between cells and organs and affect many aspects of our bodily processes. Whether we think of growth from childhood to adulthood, sexual development, mood swings, our sleep patterns or our stress management techniques, our hormones control most of these activities.

The 7 Chakras are linked with major nerve networks within the body, which workaround the glands responsible for hormone production. So working around the Chakras can influence not just your physical and mental characteristics, but your entire persona. Picture this – when you are joyful, you feel as if you are radiating happy energy onto the world; while in despair or depression, there is restriction of energy and you tend to recede into yourself. The energy movement varies under different situations and circumstances. We all commonly understand and term this movement of energy as 'e-motion' (energy in motion). This movement is characterized by actual changes in the body's chemical profile. This in turn changes the degree of muscle contractions in various organs and our neural circuitry.

The 7 chakras predominantly **deal with energy flow** in the entire body. Energy or Chakra Healing promotes healing by enhancing energy flow and correcting disturbances in the energy field of the body, thereby strengthening the emotional, mental and physical state of being.

Let me now detail the **Chakra Dhyana meditation technique** that has worked beautifully for me and most of my friends and acquaintances. It is extremely easy to follow, and effective. However, at this point, I would want to reiterate that it is advisable to start this technique under a practitioner or master for better understanding.

## THE 7 CHAKRAS

## CHAKRA DHYANA MEDITATION

The *chakra dhyana technique—chakra* meditation, helps align your chakras, clearing the way for the *kundalini shakti* to rise through them and meet Shiva. Every time you do the *dhyana*, the *kundalini shakti* rises a bit.

Balancing the chakras brings about a profound change in a person. When you change, your world will change too because the external world is a mere manifestation of your internal world. You will start noticing the changes if you continue with the processes geared to balance your chakras. One of the first changes you might observe is the way you now handle a hurt or wrong done to you. You'll find that forgiveness now comes naturally to you. Even your anger will no longer have any 'charge'. As adults, we are prone to nurse grudges against those who have hurt us. Our enemies often continue to live inside us for years. And each time we are reminded of their wrong-doing, we end up feeling the same pain all over again. But when our *chakras* are balanced, it is said, the memory might remain, but the charge will not.

As the *chakras* stand for different elements, balancing them also balances the elements in our body. Each chakra signifies a particular aspect of our lives. And it is directly connected to the brain as well. Each time a chakra gets stimulated, the corresponding part in the brain is activated. Accordingly, our thought process changes. And when thoughts change, life changes.

Most people tend to function from the lower chakras—*Muladhara, Swadhishthana* and *Manipura*. They encounter experiences of a lower order as these *chakras* are connected to the basal needs of life. The people they encounter also complement these *chakras*. They might be rich, but their thoughts remain low. When you function from the higher chakras—*Anhata, Vishuddhi* and the *Ajna,* your thought process is elevated. You attract higher life experiences, have loftier ideas, and can perceive things from a different plane. The people you meet shall be likewise.

As your *chakras* get balanced, you tend to function more from your higher chakras. Your spiritual growth then gets accelerated. Your aura starts having a positive effect on others. As you turn more positive, forgiving and enlightened, you are likely to connect better with your team, have greater foresight, and even come out with solutions that are acceptable to a majority.

**THE GUIDE TO CHAKRA DHYANA**

Every chakra has a *beeja* or core *mantra*.

The *beeja mantra* for *Muladhara chakra* is **LANG** or **LAAM**. It goes like this: **llllaaannnggggggggg...**

The *beeja mantra* for *Svadhishthana chakra* is **VANG** or **VAAM**. It goes like this: **vvvvaaannnnggggg...**

The *beeja* mantra for *Manipura chakra* is **RANG** or **RAAM.** It goes like this: **rrrraaannnggggg...**

The *beeja mantra* for *Anahata* is **YANG.** It goes like this: **yyyaaaannnggg...**

The *beeja mantra* for *Vishuddhi* is **HAANG** or **HAAM.** It goes like this: **hhhhaaaaannnngggg…**

The *beeja mantra* for *Anaya chakra* is **AUM.** It is like **AAAuuuuuuuummmmmm...**

The *beeja mantra* for *Sahasrahara chakra* is **Augum Satyam Aum.**

To remember the *Beeja mantra,* use the mnemonic **L V R Y H O**.

To do the *chakra dhyana,* sit in a comfortable position on a chair or the ground, in *padmasana* —lotus pose or *sukhasana* where you sit cross-legged, with your spine erect to facilitate the movement of the *kundalini shakti.* Ideally, meditation for each *chakra* should be done seven to ten times. But if you don't have the time, you can even meditate on one *chakra* every day.

You can do this meditation anytime. But avoid doing it immediately after lunch or dinner. On a full stomach, a feeling of heaviness is common, and also if you burp, you will find it difficult to concentrate. A slightly empty stomach can help the process. Any meditation should ideally be done in the morning as both your thoughts and the atmosphere is cleaner at this hour, and so is the mind. However, this does not imply that meditating later in the day will give less positive results; the results are independent of the timing.

Also, it is not mandatory that you bathe before meditating. You need not follow any calendar, such as the full moon or new moon. Women can do it even when they are menstruating, because this *sadhana* is not religious, but spiritual. It requires no preparations, no warm-up.

But you do need to center yourself before you start this meditation, the same as you would do in any other meditation. A distracted mind will not serve any purpose. So center your attention inwards, collect yourself and have a blissful experience.

**Remember...**

*Shiva and Shakti* are settled in the higher *chakras*. To attract higher thoughts and people, it becomes important to activate the higher *chakras* more frequently.

But first, you must activate the base or the *muladhara chakra*. Without it, you will not be able to handle the opening of any other *chakra*.

When you step on the spiritual path, the mind usually creates havoc to test you. But you will have to learn to overcome these hurdles. For instance, you might find yourself too busy and not find any time for the *dhyana.* You may just keep procrastinating for the mind refuses to let go. You then have to be strong and ask your mind to calm down. Talk to your mind; firmly explain how you will not let it stop you in your spiritual path. Practices like the *chakra* meditation can slowly deprive the mind of thoughts, which is what it feeds on. So remember, when you're performing a *sadhana,* your mind will try to distract you with thoughts. But do not try to stop these thoughts. The higher you go spiritually, the more havoc your mind will try to create. Just be aware of your thoughts and let them flow. The *chakra dhyana* yields mighty results if done on a regular basis.

Now that I have laid out a biological explanation of how the Chakras work, let me switch base to explain how the practical application of energy healing can affect day-to-day functioning, reactions and responses.

Imagine having the ability, at any given moment, to instantly uplift any aspect of your life by tapping into one of your 7 Chakras, and empowering it. Yes, it is practically possible. Whether it be in your personal or professional circle, Chakra balancing can help streamline thoughts so you can focus your energies on sharpening performance and improving relationships.

Interestingly, each of the **7 chakras control and tune certain personality traits** and influence your mindset regarding certain aspects in life. So, before you try and understand how you can balance the chakras, it is important to understand the functioning of each Chakra and its attributes.

### 1. The Root Chakra – Mooladhara

**Location: Base of the spine**

**Influence: Primarily influences your stability, survival instinct, career aspirations, money mindset and sense of belonging. Root body parts include the hips, legs, lower back and sexual organs.**

**Energies: Earth, grounding, focusing, centering**

**Beej Mantra : LANG or LAAM**

Strengthening your Root Chakra is important to feel secure and loved in your day-to-day life. The Root Chakra gives us energy to stay grounded. Our physical identity, our relationships, and our mindset towards aspirations and goals are all controlled by this Chakra. The Root Chakra also determines our self-esteem and confidence levels. When you are trying to make things happen in the material world, business or possessions, the energy to succeed will come from this chakra. The Root Chakra also impacts our vitality, passion and survival instincts. The Chakra is indicative of our need for logic and order and physical strength as well as the fight or flight response when faced with danger.

**Strong Root Chakra**

Strong Root Chakra personalities always feel loved and wanted. Even at work, these people are generally appreciated and rewarded. They are devoted to personal well-being, a comfortable home, stable family, and a secure career. If your Root Chakra is strong, you have a lot of self-confidence and do not care about judgements and opinions. You always feel good about yourself, both physically and emotionally. Root Chakra people are good at organising their assets and funds. Most of them are able to gather enough money to have a considerably comfortable lifestyle. Their greatest assets are persistence, energy and self-confidence.

## Weak Root Chakra

If your Root Chakra is weak, you often seem to be stuck in an unfulfilling and unrewarding career. People with a weak Root Chakra never seem to have enough money, which often keeps them worried and in debt. They lack the ability to budget effectively. Physically, they suffer from weight or body issues, which leaves them feeling unworthy and uncomfortable with themselves.

A weak Root Chakra person is subject to powerful physical urges which can lead to unhealthy food habits. Their fears can be easily triggered when material needs and desires aren't met. If this chakra is blocked a person may feel anxious, insecure and frustrated. Problems like obesity, anorexia and knee trouble can occur.

## 2. The Sacral Chakra – Swadhisthana

**Location: Lower abdomen**

**Influence: The Sacral Chakra influences your**

sensuality and creativity. It impacts sexuality, joy, desire and even compassion for others.

Energies: Water, energizing, charging

Beej Mantra: VANG or VAAM

This Chakra holds the basic need for creativity, intuition, and self-worth. This Chakra is also about friendliness and emotions. It governs people's sense of self-worth, their confidence and their ability to relate to others in an open and friendly way. This Chakra may be driven by how emotions were expressed or repressed during childhood. Our emotional identity is cultivated through the Sacral Chakra.

**Strong Sacral Chakra**

People with a strong Sacral Chakra are often passionate people, who make time for each other. They are always able to attract the right partners, compatible people who nourish the personality. Strong Sacral Chakra people are naturally sympathetic and attract other people. They are always in search of something new and their creativity helps them along their path. People with strong Sacral Chakras have the ability to reach higher spiritual levels of being. They can succeed as sculptors, architects, and painters.

**Weak Sacral Chakra**

If your Sacral Chakra is weak, you are barely able to make time for each other. Your partners are often incompatible, and you wonder whether you will ever find the 'right partner'. People with a weak Sacral Chakra can become aggressive and destructive and can unleash powerful energies that can harm others. Their greatest fear is the loss or abandonment of their partner. They can also experience uncontrollable jealousy. If this Chakra is blocked, a person may feel emotionally explosive and manipulative. They may lack energy. Physical problems may include kidney weakness, stiff lower back, constipation, and muscle spasms.

### 3. The Solar Plexus Chakra – Manipura

Location: Above the navel

Influence: The Solar Plexus influences your personal power and ability to channel your energies. Also influences your self-esteem.

**Energies: Fire, Energy, Charge**

**Beej Mantra: RANG or RAAM**

The Manipura Chakra is the energy center of *'doing'*. It is from this Chakra region that we find the energy to discover ourselves through exploration by taking action as unique beings. The third Chakra is the center of personal power, the place of ego, of passions, impulses, anger and strength. It is also the center for psychic development. The Solar Plexus Chakra is responsible for one's personal and professional success.

**Strong Solar Plexus Chakra**

People with a strong Solar Plexus Chakra are admired for their confidence and positive self-esteem, both in their professional and personal circles. They are never afraid to speak their mind, and empower those around them to do the same. Their family, colleagues and friends see them as charismatic individuals. Strong Solar Plexus people believe in serious pursuit of their goals and have a firm control over their thought process. They exercise great influence on the world and people around them. They have an abundant source of positive energy which ensures that they use their power for good. People with a strong Solar Plexus Chakra are often leaders. They are naturally empathetic and sensitive individuals. When this Chakra is balanced and harmonious, one feels cheerful, outgoing, confident and expressive. The element of fire allows these people to have self-respect and a strong sense of personal power. They enjoy taking on new challenges.

**Weak Solar Plexus Chakra**

You know your Solar Plexus Chakra is weak when you struggle with self-esteem issues, and are gripped by feelings of unworthiness. You are not able to accept change easily and tend to question yourself when faced with important decisions, whether it is regarding your personal or professional life. You feel like a victim in the world, and often feel powerless to circumstances and other people's desires. You may also suffer from frequent stomach pains and stomach anxiety. Sometimes, people with a weak Solar Plexus Chakra can go to extremes and use their power for personal gain. They become obsessive and disregard others. Power-hungry politicians often show these characteristics. When the third Chakra is out of balance people may also lack confidence, be confused, feel that others are controlling their life, and may be depressed. They may often report of physical problems like digestive difficulties, liver problems, diabetes, nervous exhaustion, and food allergies.

## 4. The Heart Chakra – Anahata

**Location: Centre of the chest**

**Influence:** Influences relationships and the feelings of love and self-acceptance

**Energies: Water, air, calming, soothing, relaxing**

**Beej Mantra: YANG**

This is arguably the most important of all the Chakras. The Heart Chakra directs a person's ability to love themselves and others, to give and to receive love. This is also the chakra connecting the body with the mind and spirit. It is the center of our magnetic field. We develop our social persona through the Anahata or Heart Chakra. A healthy relationship with the ego is necessary for this chakra to flourish. This Chakra helps us rise above the ego and connect with others through compassion and love.

When you are deeply hurt or face a difficult loss, there are aura obstructions called heart scars. Once the Anahata Chakra is balanced, these scars are released. This might temporarily raise a lot of old pain, but the heart becomes free for healing and positive growth.

**Strong Heart Chakra**

Love and compassion are the main characteristics of a Heart Chakra personality. You know your Heart Chakra is strong when you enjoy comfortable, loving and empathic relationships at home, at work and in your community. You get along with your family. Your friends see you as a reliable person. At work, you're known as the one people can talk to. You feel a heartfelt sense of gratitude for how wonderful your life is, and feel compassion for everything around you. Strong Heart Chakra personalities are able to make valuable contributions to help people and have great healing energy. They have the ability to make the world around them a better place. The peace in their hearts and their capacity for self-acceptance radiates a harmony that has a calming and comforting effect on others. When the Heart Chakra is balanced, you may feel compassionate, friendly, empathetic and desire to see the good in everyone.

**Weak Heart Chakra**

You know your Heart Chakra is weak when you tend to view all your relationships with distrust, doubt and anger. You always have a lingering fear that you will lose your independence if you rely too much on others. You may struggle with commitment, experience frequent fights or misunderstandings with your loved ones, and always keep yourself "on guard" in case you get hurt by someone. When this Chakra is out of balance you may feel sorry for yourself, paranoid, indecisive, afraid of letting go, afraid of getting hurt, or unworthy of love. Physical illnesses include heart attack, high blood pressure, insomnia, and difficulty in breathing. People with weak Heart Chakras often tend to be afraid of taking on too much responsibility.

## 5. The Throat Chakra – Vishuddhi

**Location: Throat**

**Influence: Influences your sense of self-expression, often referred to as the 'Chakra of your true voice'**

**Energies: Ethereal, Water, Calming, Expressive, Artistic**

**Beej Mantra: HAANG or HAAM**

One step above the Heart Chakra and located by the thyroid gland is the 'Throat Chakra'. This is where our energy for self-expression is formed. The Throat Chakra is responsible for communication, sound, and expression of creativity via thought, speech, and writing. The area of strength for the Vishuddhi Chakra is communication. Strong Throat Chakra individuals have an interest in many different things and seek knowledge at all times. They have the ability to see the patterns in life and are prone to clear thinking and true creativity. They also believe in the power of change, transformation and healing. A balanced Throat chakra allows one to move into a higher state of consciousness.

**Strong Throat Chakra**

People with a strong Throat chakra are good at voicing their thoughts, ideas and emotions to those around. They are often admired for their willpower and strong communication skills. They have the conviction to speak the truth, even though it may be uncomfortable to some. They always look for a rational explanation yet are gifted with emotional intelligence. They tend to clarify things within themselves before sharing with others. Their career and personal lives are enriched as a result. They are likely to be gifted singers and actors and can excel in areas of academia and the sciences. Individuals with a balanced Throat Chakra are able to meditate well and use their energy efficiently and artistically. When the Vishuddhi Chakra is balanced one may feel musically or artistically inspired, and may be a good speaker.

**Weak Throat Chakra**

You know your Throat Chakra is weak when you constantly feel like nobody cares about your opinions, and that you have nothing of value to say. You're likely to be known as the 'quiet one' in your professional and social circles. You frequently settle with following other people's opinions. People with a weak Throat Chakra often suffer from a blocked nose and sore throat. When this Chakra is out of balance you may want to hold back, feel timid, be quiet, feel weak, or can't express your thoughts. If this Chakra is in the overdrive mode, people may keep expressing the truth only as they see it and can have problems accepting another's point of view. They may use their gift of expression to manipulate others and often become arrogant and pretentious. Imbalance in the Vishuddhi Chakra can lead to physical ailments like hyperthyroid, skin irritations, ear infections, sore throat, inflammations, and back pain.

## 6. The Brow Chakra – Ajna

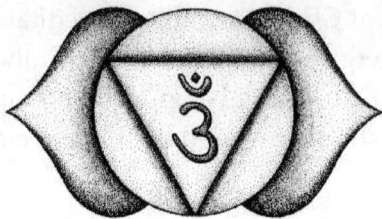

**Location: Center of the forehead**

**Influence: This Chakra acts as your inner compass. It influences your intuition.**

**Energies: Air, meditative, Intuition, Promotes thought**

**Beej Mantra: AUM**

The Third Eye or Brow Chakra is placed in the center of our brow and relates to our ability to focus and access intuition and spirituality. This is the center for the energies of spirit and light. This Chakra also assists in the purification of negative tendencies and in the elimination of selfish attitudes. A healthy third eye is believed to harness the ability to peek into a deeper realm. We are able to see ourselves as part of a bigger picture. As the Brow Chakra opens up, we begin to develop a deeper sense of purpose for a cause larger than ourselves.

## Strong Brow Chakra

Individuals with a Strong Brow Chakra are often able to make accurate intuitive decisions and evaluations about career, family or people. If your intuitive Chakra is balanced, you have a clear sense of direction and clarity in almost everything that you do. You have a vivid picture of where your life is headed, and the people around you are likely to rely on you for guidance and advice. When this Chakra is balanced and open you are not attached to material things. People with a strong Brow Chakra find fulfilment as teachers, psychologists or artists. They are also adept at healing. They seek knowledge that lies beyond the world of appearance. Their greatest quest is true wisdom. They experience inner peace and can radiate positive energy. They can be intensely creative and it is a natural occurrence for them. They have an innate ability to recognize lies and delusions, and can avoid these pitfalls.

## Weak Brow Chakra

You know your Brow Chakra is weak if you feel lost and helpless when faced with decisions and judgment calls. You are indecisive, uncommitted and not confident of the decisions you end up making, because you have a history of making the wrong ones. You feel spiritually lost, and your true purpose is unclear to you. You often get headaches and feel tension in your brow area. When the Brow Chakra is weak, you tend to lose contact with the material world, thereby distancing yourself from others. This can lead to isolation and depression. When this Chakra is not balanced you may feel non-assertive, afraid of success, or go the opposite way and be egotistical. Physical symptoms may include headaches, blurred vision and eye strain.

## 7. The Crown Chakra – Sahasrahara

**Location: Top of the head**

**Influence: This is the Chakra of divine consciousness. It influences your connection to the Universe.**

**Energies: Air, Meditative, Intuition, Dynamic thought, Wisdom.**

**Beej Mantra: Augum Satyam Aum**

The Crown Chakra is the highest chakra on the chart and relates to our feelings of oneness with all things, often described as universal identity. This Chakra is the basis for true self-knowledge and a greater sense of inner divinity. Barely a few of us will ever get to reach this stage throughout our lives since achieving this state requires a vibrating and healthy chakra system as a whole.

**Strong Crown Chakra**

When your Crown Chakra is strong, you feel perpetually connected to a higher power; whether you call it God, the Universe or simply your higher self. As you go through your daily life, you are always reminded that you are being watched over, and feel immense gratitude for the universal love and appreciation towards yourself and others. People with a strong Crown Chakra seek liberation towards the highest level of self-realization. Their experiences and perceptions are so different from others that they sometimes come off as being incomprehensible. In fact, they can often be misunderstood. They can succeed in any chosen profession; however they are often in areas of spiritual leadership. They have an unconditional striving for perfection. They let nothing stand in the way of their goal. They radiate energy that effects positive transformations in those around them. In its balanced state, the Crown Chakra can give individuals the ability to have a heightened sense of awareness about life.

**Weak Crown Chakra**

You know your Crown Chakra is weak when you feel little or no connection to a higher power, and always feel alone. You feel lost and perhaps even angry that you have nothing or no one to help or guide you. People with a weak Crown Chakra are prone to superstition and drawn to negative energies. When this Chakra is unbalanced there may be a constant sense of frustration, no spark of joy, and destructive feelings. Weak Crown Chakra individuals often want to withdraw from the world and can practice extreme self-denial. Illnesses may include migraine headaches and depression.

## CHAKRA BALANCING AND HEALING

Now that we have charted out the nuances of each Chakra and its psychological and physiological undertones, it is easier to understand how 'Chakra Balancing' can bring about a change, not only in our thought process but also our physical well-being.

It is a true fact that most of us react to unpleasant experiences by blocking our feeling and stopping a great deal of our natural energy flow. This affects the functioning of the Chakras. Whenever a person blocks an experience he/she is having, he in turn blocks his energies that affect the 'Chakras', which eventually become disfigured. The imbalances that exist within any Chakra may have profound effects on one's physical or emotional body.

If the energies are blocked, you may feel tired, out of sorts, or even depressed. Not only will physical or bodily functions be affected, but the entire thought, reaction and response process will be affected. You will slowly begin to develop a negative attitude towards life, full of fear, doubt and worry.

Once the Chakras open up, you will naturally start to feel relaxed, energetic, healthy and blissful. The principle is simple. When the Chakras are balanced, they have the capacity to pull particular energies from the universal energy field that can be used for healing.

In my forthcoming chapters, I will lay out a detailed 'Chakra Chart' to better understand what physical and behavioral aspect each Chakra controls and regulates. I will also present simple little exercises to try and activate each underactive Chakra. However, in my opinion, it would be ideal to have a few sessions with a Chakra expert initially, so you are able to gather inputs on your active and underactive Chakras and work on a healing process that leads to effective balance.

For most of us, it may seem easy to dismiss the idea of Chakra Science altogether, especially if you have a questioning mind. I have shared my doubts as well, but after practical application, I would surely recommend that you take time to see how Energy Healing relates to science and its principles. Take your own personal experience and come up with rational arguments to help your understanding. My bottom line would be, adopt the "why not" approach rather than the "why". Believe me, the benefits will amaze you.

*Air moves us, Fire transforms us, Water shapes us and the Earth heals us. Connect with  the elements and you will be able to understand better.'*

# CHAPTER 12
# THE 5 ELEMENTS

————◆◆————

Since we are out to explore ways of synchronizing our bodily energies with the infinite pool of Universal Energy, let me bring into the picture another crucial component that you will need to connect with in order to expand and harmonize your relationship with all things, physical and metaphysical – The 5 elements.

The Five Subtle Elements - Earth, Fire, Water, Air and Ether or Space form the basis for all things found in the material creation, from a grain of sand to the complex physiology of every human being.

The elements or the Pancha Maha Bhutas as the Vedas describe them are the fundamental building blocks of the Universe. These 5 elements are the essence of the entire world, both within you and outside, so it is more than essential to connect with them for tapping into the powers of the Universe. It might seem rather surprising but the 5 elements also influence our behaviour, emotions, and overall health. Balancing these elements in just the right way is the key to a happy and healthy life. If we take some time to understand the elements and relate to them, we can use them to stay in balance physically, spiritually, emotionally and mentally.

By understanding the positive and negative aspects of each element, we can tune our minds to use each element in the most effective way. The first rule of thumb is that we cannot dominate the elements. Instead, we have to surrender to the elements and respect them. The more we comprehend the Pancha Mahabhutas, the more we will understand and relate to the universe. The best way to get to grips with these 5 elements is to figure out their basic characteristics and how they relate to physical attributes. Here is a simple way to begin your journey of understanding the universe from an element-based viewpoint.

## THE FIVE ELEMENTS (Pancha Mahabhutas)

### EARTH

The Earth element is the most powerful of all elements. The Earth is our source of stability. Earth represents balance and dominates Center and Diagonal directions. When it is in a balanced state, it induces a feeling of stability, peace and harmony. In human attributes, strengthening the Earth element enhances the strength of mind, steadfastness, determination and uninterrupted advancement towards a goal.

To strengthen the Earth element, you can try these simple steps:

✫ Make sure that you 'Thank the Earth' wholeheartedly every day when you wake up in the morning. Thank the fact that you are standing on Mother Earth that supports so many life forms. As soon as you get up, touch Mother Earth, touch your forehead and ask for her blessings to keep you grounded through the day.

✫ Be mindful of what you are doing each moment as the day passes. Focus your attention on deep-rooted breathing. Your breathing should be full in the belly (stomach expands on breathing in, contracts on breathing out).

✫ Keep well grounded - always feel your feet on the ground, or the bottom on your chair.

✫ Stay in touch with the physical experience of walking, standing or sitting on the ground, sometime during the day.

✫ Practice disciplines such as yoga or martial arts that work as a means of connecting to Mother Earth.

## WATER

—✵❦❧✵—

The Water element is a huge life force. Water is also known to have healing powers. Almost 70% of the earth and our bodies are made up of water. Water has nurturing energies. We can observe perfect cycles of water throughout the planet. You must have realized that when you take a bath, or go swimming, the body naturally relaxes very quickly. Water pulls out negativity, balances our emotions, and makes our mind calm and focused. When water is in a balanced state, it induces a spiritual and philosophical attitude to life. In attributes, Water is associated with the power of conceptualising new ideas, thoughts, healing energy and restoration of health. It also has an effect on emotions, feelings and intuition.

To strengthen the Water element:

✵ Drink loads of water through the day. This may sound simple, but according to dieticians, many of us go around in a state of partial dehydration every day. To add to it, the intake of tea, coffee and juices uses up some of the body's water to be digested. So it is essential to keep drinking enough water to keep yourself hydrated and energetic through the day. It is vital for good health.

✴ Since the water element controls emotions, it is important to let your feelings flow freely like water. Learn to acknowledge and respect all your feelings without labeling them as good or bad, negative or positive. Express as much as you can. Try and share your feelings with anyone you feel close to or can trust.

✴ Practice a listening sensitivity to other people's feelings as well.

✴ Avoid added sugars. These sugars interfere with the absorption of anthocyanin pigments that help in keeping the kidneys safe and active.

✴ Practice being introspective and listen to your body. Focus on recharging your reserves. Examine your daily routine. Study what leaves you feeling great and what leaves you drained. Try to balance your routine so you pull time out for doing what makes your mind happy or peaceful.

✴ Water also has the capacity to hold energy. Use a copper vessel to store water overnight so it is able to pull out positive energies. Drink this water early in the morning.

✴ Try and practice swimming. It is a great activity to soothe and heal the body and mind.

## FIRE

Fire is the driving force behind all life processes. When in a balanced state, Fire induces power, confidence, fame, recognition and money. The Fire element is the element of love and all affairs of the heart. Fire represents our relationship with our self and with others. It governs our ability to share love, warmth and joy with friends, colleagues, intimate partners, and in fact with the entire human race. It is the spark inside that allows us to feel enthusiastic and inspired in what we do. Opening and enriching the mind to recognize the power of Fire or the Sun is a great generator for all creation. Fire is associated with Universal energy, as also with the inner guiding light that helps destroy all doubts and negative thoughts. The Fire element is worshipped in various forms across religions. The Sun aptly represents this element. Sunlight sustains life, it brightens and illuminates. The early morning sun can heal many diseases and depression. Fire brings with it a lot of positive energy and power.

Fire in its positive form is enlightenment and radiance, however, it can also result in negative traits like rage, hatred, greed, envy, and the desire for revenge. So it is very important to connect with the Fire element and keep it balanced. Learning to regulate and temper your inner fire is essential for moving ahead in life with zest.

In traits, individuals with a balanced Fire element are often capable of clear, perceptive, and discriminating judgment. They can digest and synthesize large amounts of information. They can be extremely focused, working relentlessly towards their goals. They however, deliver their judgments in scathing attacks, and love to argue and win. They are articulate.

Though Fire is one of the strongest elements, it is the hardest to balance. Here are a few suggestions on what you can do to stabilize your Fire element:

✴ If you have an east-facing window, open it at sunrise, letting in as much of the early morning light as possible. If you can sit out in the sun and let the rays touch your body, better still.

✴ Ensure that you worship the power of Fire in any form during the day. Thank the Sun for providing you the energy to run through the day.

✴ Use soft-scented candles around the house.

✴ Bring warm lighting and colours into your home.

✴ Wear more warm colours - reds, oranges, yellows.

✴ Drop the cynicism and train yourself to see the bright side of every event.

✴ Go on a brisk walk.

✴ Make time for creative self-expression.

✶ Find healthy ways to burn off nervous energy.

✶ Non-competitive swimming is an excellent exercise to soothe the Fire element and keep it under check.

## AIR

The Air element is our most basic connection to life. Our body can only survive if we breathe. Air represents growth and is associated with movement, joy and happiness. When in a balanced state, Air induces courage and perseverance to achieve your goals.

While balancing the Air element, it is important to understand that each of us breathes the same air, even plants and animals. This makes it easier to connect to the thought that we are all one. That we are all the same, only our surroundings, upbringing and circumstances frame us. Once you connect to this thought, you can easily connect with everyone and stop finding faults and imperfections in others. When the Air element is balanced, the mind is peaceful and controlled. By mastering the mind, you also gain the capacity to handle all other elements and use their energies to the best advantage.

Much like Fire, unless kept under check, the Air element has the capacity to bring in nervous agitation, fear, and anxiety. Once balanced, Air can positively initiate new insights, revelations and knowledge. Air activates inspiration and creativity. Once you connect to the Air element, your sense of intuition also grows stronger.

The Air element can be balanced in various ways:

- ✯ Resolve to wake up early to allow ample time for all the things that need to get done before the work day commences.
- ✯ Get outdoors for a morning walk or other exercise and fill your lungs, eyes and ears with the clarity and peace that the morning offers.
- ✯ A period of meditation, prayer or yoga will help cement the feeling of centeredness and peace before the craziness of the work day begins.
- ✯ Cut down on caffeine and other stimulants.
- ✯ Don't skip a meal, and take time to eat slowly.
- ✯ Spend some time watching clouds float around in the sky.
- ✯ Spend time bird watching.
- ✯ Try out Breathing Meditation (following your breath)
- ✯ Design a daily routine that creates stability, calm, and peace.

✳ Once dinner is done, wind down toward a peaceful night of sleep.

✳ Take a break from the information deluge.

✳ Stop fidgeting with your cell phone.

✳ Steer clear of anxiety-inducing images and news, especially at night.

## SPACE

The element of Space represents expansion and enhancement. When it is in a balanced state, it induces knowledge and awareness to understand new and creative ideas. The Space element encompasses everything around us and influences the mind and the heart. Enhancing the Space element helps you smoothly sync your energies with the Universal energies.

Also referred to as Ether, the influence of the Space element is limitless. Balancing the Space element can in fact give you the highest self-healing powers. You can heal anything from addictions and heartbreak, to depression. The Space element is most powerful and dominant because without the Akash Tatva, none of the other 4 elements can exist. If there is no Space, nothing can exist. So it is crucial that we get up every morning and thank Space for supporting life and all life forms, including us.

Here are some simple ways to keep the Ether energies balanced:

✵ Try and surround yourself with the colour blue. This colour is associated with the Ether element.

✵ While meditation or prayer, sit silently and feel the expanse of Space. Connect with the sounds of the Universe. Feel the peace.

✵ Engage in some form of Art or Music.

✵ Travel a lot. Learn and Explore.

✵ Focus on the sense of hearing, whether to conversations, responses or the sounds of nature.

✵ Spend time with literature/music/movies/images that inspire you on a regular basis.

✵ Consciously practise 'Big Picture' thinking. Expand your horizon from carrying through day-to-day activities to thinking about the larger purpose and rhythm of Life.

Now that we have explored a few characteristics of the Five Elements, let me draw your attention to another interesting fact. Most of us know that human beings cognize the physical world through five essential sensory organs. But what is not so widely known is the fact that each of these senses is related to one of the five elements: ether, air, fire, water, and earth.

The Earth element is related to the sense of smell. Water is related to the organ of taste because without water the tongue cannot taste. Fire manifests light, heat and color and is related to vision. Air is related to the sense of touch, the sensory organ of touch being the skin, and Ether or Space is the medium through which sound is transmitted, thus the ethereal element is related to the hearing function.

The Five Elements represent the universe of matter-energy. Any imbalance in these five elements creates disease in the human body. The aim of strengthening and balancing the elements is to correct internal and external imbalance and ensure a healthy, peaceful and stress-free life.

Beyond the 5 elements, it is also crucial to understand and revere the fundamentals of 'The Soul' (Atma) and 'Consciousness' (Atman) that we also term as elements. The 5 known elements along with the soul and consciousness are what compose life. Every action originates from the soul and is given meaning by consciousness. Consciousness is universal in animate or inanimate objects. Everything, even beyond the earth's surface, has consciousness. The planets that move around the sun, the sun and moon, objects in space, everything has consciousness. The soul adds meaning and expression to that all-pervasive consciousness. However, though the soul can get fragmented, consciousness cannot. It is just there, ever-present, all-encompassing. The Atma and Atman are interdependent and give meaning to life. The Ajna or Third Eye Chakra houses the Soul and the Sahasrahara or Crown Chakra houses Consciousness.

As important as it is to connect with the elements, it is also important to conform to the **'Pancha Sutras' or the five lessons of Life.** Let me elaborate.

**1. Perform Right Action –** Do your duties or any action that you are doing without any guilt or emotional burden. Whether in the professional or personal circle, do what you are doing happily and the results will change for the positive.

**2. Break the Barrier –** The Universe always helps you when you break the barrier. Most of us do not have faith in the Universe so we don't ask for help. Try, and the Universe will offer help. Never say that you cannot do a thing – you will never evolve. Never go by pre-set norms and ideas, never go by what others think or say. Learn to break your own barriers and ask for help.

**3. Grow by 'Giving' –** By this, I mean, 'Giving' not only in material terms. You can Give Knowledge, Give Love, Smiles, Support, Compassion, and Understanding. That is when real transformation will happen. When you stretch yourself a little bit, you will take baby steps from 'I' to 'You'. Do not expect anything in return. Give whole-heartedly, have faith and the Universe will give back. Life is an Echo. If you say I Love you, the universe will respond and say I love you. Love will multiply.

**4. Set your Goals** – Long term or short term, set goals for yourself and keep accomplishing them. But do not expect quick marvels. Keep pushing towards your goals slowly and gently and they will be accomplished. Through life's way, these goals will also keep you happy and engrossed. Also remember you will always reach your goal if you put your heart into whatever you are doing.

**5. Connect with the Divine** – Learn to connect with and tap into the Energy pool of the Universe. If you are uncomfortable with the word 'Divine' or 'God', you are free to term it anything from cosmic to universal energy. Connect with that energy. Cosmic help will come to you provided you ask for it. In meditation and prayer, focus on asking for help. In practicality, work out solutions. Do not over expect, but trust in the powers of the Universe and answers will come to you.

Remember, our external sense organs enable us to interact with the material objects of the world. However, they have to be supported by the five elements to receive finer knowledge and connect to the infinite powers of the Universe. The combined operation of these two along with the Pancha Sutras or 5 lessons of Life will not only help you transform inside out but lead you towards a life of complete peace and bliss. It's surely worth a try!

*'The true return to Nature is a definitive
return to the Elements.'*

# Chapter 13
## Element-Based Chakra Healing

—————◆◆◆—————

The Universe has some unique hidden marvels. An interesting fact, amongst many, is that the five elements of Earth, Air, Water, Fire, and Ether correspond to the Chakras or Energy centers in the human body. All five elements exist to a certain degree within each of the 7 Chakras. Each Chakra contains a 'layer' of the five elemental levels of energy. In fact, each is endowed with the capacity to awaken certain powerful features.

1. The Muladhara chakra or Root Chakra represents stability and support. It indicates Earth element.

2. Swadishthan or Sacral chakra represents joy and general sense of well-being. It indicates Water element.

3. Manipura or Solar Plexus chakra represents power and wisdom. It indicates Fire element.

4. Anahata or Heart chakra represents love, forgiveness, compassion to all. It indicates Air element.

5. Vishuddha or Throat chakra represents faith in our selves, trust in others, creativity. It indicates Ether element.

6. Ajna or Brow chakra represents knowledge, dignity and intuition. It indicates Ether element.

7. Sahasrahara or Crown chakra represents perfect balance, oneness with the universe. It indicates Ether element.

Each element interacts with the Chakras to create different functions and structures. Balancing of the Chakras through the elements is therefore extremely important for progression and harmony. The 3 Lower chakras are connected to the external or outer world so the colours are bold – Red, Orange, Yellow. The Upper 4 chakras are connected to the inner world and the colours are lighter. Apart from colour and sound, each of the seven chakras have their own unique elements. The related Crystal – Metal – Colour and Mantra together form an energy grid, working around which can help heal physical discomfort or mental disturbance. Visualization with the associated chakra colour while using its respective sound can deepen and amplify the experience.

| NAME | COLOR | MANTRA | LOCATION | ELEMENT | GLAND | DIETY | ANGEL | VIRTUE | METAL |
|---|---|---|---|---|---|---|---|---|---|
| Root Chakra | Red | Laang | Perineum | Earth | Adrenal | Ganesha | Sandalphon | Stability/ Survival | Gold |
| Sacral Chakra | Orange | Vaang | Genitals | Water | Gonads | Vishnu | Chamuel | Pleasures | Silver |
| Solar Plexus | Yellow | Raang | Navel | Fire | Pancreas | Maharudra Shiva | Uriel | Importance/ Significance | Steel |
| Heart Chakra | Green | Yaang | Heart Center | Air | Thymus | Ishvara | Raphael | Love/ To be loved | Zinc |
| Throat Chakra | Blue | Haang | Throat | Space | Thyroid | Sadashiva | Michael | Surrender/ Acceptance | Tin |
| Third Eye | Indigo | Om | Center of eyebrows | – | Pituitary | Ardhanaresh wara | Gabriel | Wisdom/ Intellect | Copper |
| Crown Chakra | Violet | Om | Top of the head | – | Pineal | Lord Shiva | Zadkiel | Oneness | Lead |

# ACTIVATING THE 7 CHAKRAS - SIMPLE EXERCISES

## MOOLADHARA (ROOT) CHAKRA – PERINEUM – RED- EARTH - LAANG

The Mooladhara Chakra is based in the tailbone. Interestingly, this is the last organ of the body to disintegrate once a person dies because it is the strongest nucleus where the Kundalini Shakti resides. It is crucial to balance the Mooladhara Chakra because it forms the base for all relationships, life and work. Mooladhara is a fear-based Chakra. It controls the adrenalin rush whenever there are extreme situations. Imbalance in this Chakra can bring about anxiety, panic, a feeling of being left out, financial insecurity and in extreme cases result in severe 'Depression'. Since the colour of the Mooladhara Chakra is Red, to bring about balance, try and place more reds around the house. Even for personal use, ladies can try and using red handbags, red bangles and red coloured clothing. Men can use red t-shirts and accessories like red pens and laptop covers.

The Mooladhara Chakra is dominated by the Earth element. With changing lifestyles, most of us have lost connection with Mother Earth. We barely sit or sleep on the floor. Each of our needs is taken care of by the Earth but we barely acknowledge it. So, as step 1, get into the habit of touching the floor and putting your hand on your forehead, acknowledging and respecting the amount the Earth is doing for us, each and every day. Connecting with the Earth is very important to activate the Mooladhara Chakra.

**Exercises for balancing the Mooladhara:**

**Exercise 1**

Sit on the floor in a 'Butterfly' pose, bringing the base of the feet together. Place your hands firmly on the ground on either side of your body and move your bottom up and down, rising and coming down slowly. This exercise needs to be done about 5-10 times every day.

**Exercise 2**

When the Mooladhara Chakra is shaken, even the Foot Chakra gets damaged. For activating this, sit down on a chair and join both the feet together, completing the Chakra. Then activate it by stomping gently on the floor.

As a variation, you can stomp each foot on the floor 4-5 times. Try and do this exercise at various points during the day. You can also try marching in one place.

**Exercise 3**

Before you wind down for the day, lie flat on the floor with your back touching the ground. Try and run through the happenings of the day, balancing the good and not-so-good events. End with thinking about all the little things that made you happy, even the small little chocolate that you ate after dinner. Then lie still, affirming to yourself, 'I am Safe and Secure. I am firm and grounded. I am one with the Earth'. Feel the heaviness of your body sink into the Earth. Think about how you are rooted firmly with the Earth and imagine the Earth energy being able to flow up through you. During the process, do not forget to thank Mother Earth for having supported you through the day. This root chakra exercise will help you feel grounded and grateful, stabilizing you mentally and physically.

## SWADISTHAN (SACRAL) CHAKRA – GONADS – ORANGE- WATER - VAANG

The Swadisthan Chakra is a fluid, emotion-based chakra. It represents sexuality, creativity, joy and general sense of wellness. Most sexual problems arise because of an imbalance in the Swadisthan Chakra. Menstrual irregularity, Infertility, low conception rate, erectile Dysfunction or one of the most common problems in women, of PCOD, can be controlled by balancing the Swadisthan Chakra.

The Sacral Chakra is also tied to our ability to experience pleasure and express our emotions in a healthy way. Suppressing too many emotions can also lead to an imbalance in the Chakra.

Though learning to let go is a difficult task, it is essential for balancing the Swadisthan Chakra. Try simply talking with a close friend about things that are bothering you on the personal or professional front. If that seems tough, consider journaling what you feel inside, jotting down emotions as they flow. Do not try and format your thoughts. You will be amazed to see how much better you feel when you vocalize or let go of repressed emotions and experiences.

Since the Swadisthan Chakra is driven by the water element, swimming is one activity that is highly recommended to bring about balance in the Chakra. You might have realised that most of us feel a sense of calm whenever we are near a water body. This is because water has the capacity to both churn and soothe emotions. Water dominates the aspects which are adaptable, penetrating, dissolving, mobile, and flowing. You can also work with the colour Orange, associated with the Chakra. Try and introduce subtle to bright shades of orange in your office and home decor. Add a touch of warming orange to your wardrobe. You can also try introducing some earthy orange tones to your jewellery and accessories.

**Exercises for balancing the Swadisthan:**

**Exercise 1**

Stand in a comfortable position with the legs slightly apart. Put your hands on the waist and twist your torso round and round, imagining as if you are inside a hula hoop. Go around in one direction 5 or 6 times and then switch directions from left to right and right to left.

**Exercise 2**

In a seated position, bring the bottom of your feet together. Let your knees drop to the sides. Bring your heels in closer to your pelvis. Lengthen the torso and bend forward. Keep in this pose for a count of five and then release. Repeat about 4-5 times.

**Exercise 3**

Sit on the floor with your legs spread out as wide as possible. Flex your feet with toes facing upwards. Contract your thigh muscles to lift your kneecaps up towards your hips. Then, place your hands on the floor behind you, with the palm and fingers facing forward. Hold this position till a count of 10 and then release slowly. Repeat about 2-3 times.

## MANIPURA (SOLAR PLEXUS) CHAKRA – NA-VEL – YELLOW- FIRE - RAANG

The Fire element manifests in our body as heat in the Solar Plexus or the Manipura Chakra. This Chakra controls our energy balance to strengthen and consolidate our health. The pancreas controls this Chakra so lot of issues like digestion, bile production, sugar, high BP and cholesterol can be controlled by balancing the Manipura Chakra. Once the Manipura Chakra is balanced, stomach-related problems, heart problems and weight issues can be kept under check, thereby promoting better health.

Fire dominates the Manipura Chakra. Considered one of the strongest elements, Fire goes against the gravitational force and pull. In most religions, Fire is worshipped and considered sacred. Hindus believe that Fire can take your message straight up to God in the form of its flames. That is why Havans have been promoted as an effective form of prayer. To bring balance to the Manipura Chakra, which is controlled by the Fire element, you can try conducting the 'Om Prabhu Shanti Havan'. It is a simple Havan that can be done by you at home, any time of the day (check details on You Tube by typing 'Om Prabhu Shanti Havan'. Lighting of candles, agarbattis and dhoop around the house or work area can also cleanse the area and enhance performance.

There are a few precautions with food that you can observe to help balance the Manipura Chakra:

* Drink beverages at room temperature or slightly warmed. Avoid too much ice.

* Make an approximate portion for every meal. Eat about two cupped handfuls of food to avoid overeating.

* Stay away from highly spicy foods.

* Take small sips of water while eating. Avoid soda and fruit juices with food. Drinking a lot while eating tends to dilute the digestive acids.

* Let your stomach rest between meals. Grazing and frequent snacking does not give your body time to replenish hunger.

**Exercises for balancing the Manipura:**

**Exercise 1**

Stand comfortably with the legs slightly split. Put your hands on the waist and bob the waist back and front, not sideways or around. Make sure that there is no pressure or pain on the back. This exercise will help strengthen your digestive system.

**Exercise 2**

Since the third Chakra governs both digestion and metabolism, simple breathing exercises also work effectively to balance the Manipura. Ensure that your stomach is not full before starting any breathing exercise.

Sit comfortably with the spine pulled up tall and the shoulders relaxed. Start by taking a few deep breaths in and out of the nose with the lips closed. Then, forcefully inhale through the nose while inflating the lower abdomen and forcefully exhale through the nose while pressing the lower abdomen toward the spine. Use one and a half count on the inhalation and one and a half count on the exhalation. Try for 10 repetitions and then work it up to 15 or 20. After you're finished, you will feel a tingling or glowing feeling around the navel.

You can also try a variation by standing erect, trying to breathe in and out sharply, pulling the stomach in as you breathe in and out as you breathe out.

**Exercise 3**

Sit up with the legs stretched out straight in front of you, keeping the feet together and the spine erect. Take the right leg over the left knee. Place the left hand on the right knee and the right hand behind you. Twist the waist, shoulders and neck in this sequence to the right and look over the right shoulder. Keep the spine erect. Hold and continue with gentle long breaths in and out. Breathing out, release the right hand first (the hand behind you), release the waist, then chest, lastly the neck and sit up relaxed. Repeat to the other side. Breathing out, come back to the front and relax.

## ANAHATA (HEART) CHAKRA – CENTRE OF THE CHEST – GREEN- AIR - YAANG

The Anahata or Heart Chakra is the first Chakra that is responsible for bringing about internal balance rather than controlling external or physiological symptoms and functions. The need to love and be loved arises from this Chakra. The Anahata Chakra is controlled by the Thymus gland. This gland is very active in kids but slowly, as we age, it becomes less active. The Heart Chakra is usually dormant in adults so it needs to be worked on and tapped. Sometimes if the Heart Chakra becomes over-active, it can result in people becoming over-possessive. But if it is under-active, it could make one cold towards all relationships and often stone-hearted. It is crucial to keep the Heart Chakra balanced for smooth personal and professional relationships. A balanced Anahata Chakra will not only make you feel wanted and loved, it will make you open-hearted and accommodating, and help you experience not only attachment with near and dear ones but universal love for each and every soul around. You will be able to get rid of biases, judgements, harsh feelings or bitterness, and have very few enemies. The Heart Chakra is driven by the element of Air. There is movement and freshness in air and the same stands true for the Anahata Chakra. Once the Heart Chakra flowers, you begin to experience inner peace and calm. The heart opens up to a feeling of Universal love and brotherhood and there is extreme freedom in whatever you think and do. When the Fourth Chakra is open and balanced, it fosters forgiveness and gives rise to unconditional love.

**Exercises for balancing the Anahata:**

**Exercise 1**

Whenever you find yourself under tension or are extremely excited, worried or anxious, gently tap the centre of your rib cage, just a bit below your throat, with your fingertips. This exercise helps soothe and activate the Heart Chakra. You will start to feel calm and relaxed within a few moments of doing this exercise.

**Exercise 2**

Doing push-ups or swimming (especially the breast stroke) is a good therapy for balancing the Heart Chakra.

**Exercise 3**

Lie upside down on your stomach, with legs stretched out behind. The feet can be slightly apart.

Place your hands directly under the shoulders with palms pressing against the ground. Slowly and gently arch the back, lifting the chest upward. The shoulders should be kept away from the ears and neck. The arms and elbows need to be held tight against the sides. Then press the pubic bone into the ground to support the lower body and lift the head, shoulders and chest off the floor. Hold the pose for about 5 counts. To come out of the pose, slowly lower your shoulders, chest, and abdomen down towards the floor. This exercise is also known as the cobra pose.

**Exercise 4**

The best way to receive love is to give love. Hug all those around whom you would want to pass on your love to, and make sure that you pull a few precious hugs for yourself too. Take any opportunity you can to foster love and loving feelings. Smile at everyone you see, even if sometimes you don't feel like smiling. It's contagious. Give friends, family and co-workers positive affirmations and feedback. Try to go one day a week without criticizing anyone or anything, including yourself. Forgive and move on. Life is too short to hold grudges. Keep repeating this positive affirmation to yourself and see the stark change it brings about in your perspective of everything around, 'Love is everywhere. Love is the purpose of my life, and I will give and receive loads of love in this journey of life'.

## VISHUDDHA (THROAT) CHAKRA – THYROID – BLUE- SPACE- HAANG

The Vishuddha or Throat Chakra controls your speech and oratory skills externally. Internally, a balanced Throat Chakra heightens the feeling of acceptance and surrender to the Universe. From a professional point of view, balancing the Throat Chakra is vital for those from the field of marketing, actors and performers. If the Vishuddha is not balanced, you may find it tough to effectively express yourself, or be able to listen to others, even to your own higher self. Too much alcohol, smoking, drugs, and overeating can damage the Throat Chakra. This can manifest as neck stiffness, shoulder tension, and teeth-grinding. An imbalance can also create feelings of anxiety, insecurity, and shyness when it comes to self-expression or speaking to others.

As opposed to Air that symbolises the Heart Chakra, the element of Space symbolises the Vishuddha Chakra. Though there is no movement in Space but vacuum and stillness, nothing can exist if there is no Space. So it is essential that we always remain thankful to Space. We all exist because of the creation of Space.

The colour that represents the Throat Chakra is Blue. Enhanced usage of the colour in and around the house and items of personal use can bring inspiration, self-expression, creativity and trust in the self and others.

**There are also a few simple steps that can help balance the Vishuddha Chakra:**

✴ Make a conscious effort to drink more water throughout the day. Water cleanses the Throat Chakra, allowing for healthy energy flow.

✴ Add apples, peaches, lemons and limes to your diet to cleanse and activate the Throat Chakra.

✴ Aromatherapy can help restore balance to the Chakras. Consider introducing a combination of jasmine, rosemary, sandalwood, calendula and ylang ylang oils to heal and activate your Throat Chakra.

✴ Talk and express yourself to family and close friends. Make it a point to be open and honest. Speaking openly in a heartfelt way can work wonders to strengthen and balance the Throat Chakra.

✴ Learn how to express yourself without censoring or editing. Practice mindful self-expression by maintaining a daily diary. Get it all out on paper and let it sit, then revisit what you have written at a later time.

✴ Letting go is one of the toughest things to do. However, holding on to things over which you have no control can lead to resentment, guilt, and anger, all of which contribute to an imbalance of the Throat Chakra. So JUST LET GO.

**Exercises for balancing the Vishuddha:**

**Exercise 1 – Ujjai Pranayam – Breathing in and out through the throat**

Inhale deeply through the nose. Slightly contract the throat and exhale through the throat so that the breath sounds like that in deep sleep. Direct your attention completely on the throat. This way of breathing will quieten the mind and balance emotions. Ujjai Pranayam detoxifies the body and helps with problems of the digestive system, especially gastritis. Because of its effect on the thyroid gland, regular practice of this Pranayam makes you feel healthy and rejuvenated. This breathing exercise is also very helpful for relieving depression.

**Exercise 2 - Simha Mudra**

Sit in the basic Vajrasana pose and spread your knees. Your spine should be straight but relaxed. The hands should be kept straight in between your legs. Now inhale and take out your tongue. Try to look between in the eyebrows and exhale. During exhaling, roar loudly like a lion with the sound 'Haa'. After roaring, hold the sitting pose for 20 to 30 seconds. Repeat this process about 4 to 6 times.

**Exercise 3**

Exhale, placing your hands on the knees. Tilt the body forward slightly and press the chin down onto the sternum. Hold this position for as long as is comfortable, and when the impulse to inhale occurs release the position by raising the head. You will feel a sudden, increased flow of fresh blood in the throat region once the exhaling position is released.

**Exercise 4**

Gargling with salt water or drinking warm water before and after a meal can also help clear the Throat Chakra. Reading aloud or singing also helps in releasing blockages and activating the Throat Chakra.

## AJNA (THIRD EYE) CHAKRA – PITUITARY / PINEAL - INDIGO - OM

The Ajna or Third Eye Chakra controls our intellect and wisdom. The 6th Chakra deals with the workings of our higher mind, intuition, and imagination. If the Ajna Chakra is balanced, you can make wise and quick decisions, and live a healthy life with positivity, understanding and love. If the Chakra is under active, you feel lost and helpless. If it goes into over-drive mode, you stop being a learner and start developing spiritual ego. A blocked Third Eye can wreak havoc on your physical and psychological well-being. Since this energy centre governs your pituitary gland and neurological function, it can affect your body's ability to fight infection, regulate sleep, and maintain balanced metabolic function. You may also suffer from migraines, sinusitis, poor vision or sciatica. In extreme cases, an imbalance can lead to a stroke or blindness. You could also experience delusions, depression, anxiety, paranoia or heightened scepticism.

Embracing compassion and forgiveness is essential to successful clearing and healing of the Ajna Chakra. Awakening of the Chakra helps cope with problems relating to the brain. It is helpful for dealing with psychic problems such as depression, schizophrenia or changeable emotions. The Third Eye is instrumental in your ability to visualize. So the most effective technique for balancing the Ajna Chakra lies in meditation.

**Exercises for balancing the Ajna:**

**Exercise 1**

**Chanting of 'Om'** - Brain power and focus can be increased by proper chanting of the sound "OM". Om is the universal sound, the first sound that emerged in the Universe, so it is very strong and powerful. Chanting "OM" will **break loose the constraints that you have imposed by not listening to your inner wisdom** and direct it to chart a better course of life.

**Exercise 2**

The Bhramari style Pranayama helps alleviate tension and works well to open the Sixth Chakra. For this exercise, bring both hands to your face. Place the two middle fingers over your eyes. Allow the index fingers to rest on the eyebrow line and the pinky fingers under the cheekbones. Close your ears with your thumbs. Take a deep inhalation and exhale the word 'OM' while creating a buzzing sound like a bee. Do this for two or three minutes.

**Exercise 3**

Kneel down on the floor and touch your big toes to each other as you sit on your heels. Then spread your knees hip-width apart. Inhale. Bend forward, and lay your torso between your thighs as you exhale. Stretch your arms forward and place them in front of you, such that they are in line with your knees. Release the front of your shoulders to the floor. You must feel the weight of the front shoulders pulling the blades widely across your back. You can stay in the pose from anywhere between 30 seconds to a few minutes.

**Exercise 4**

Aromatherapy, the use of Chakra stones, or sound therapy, can help restore balance to the Third Eye chakra. Also ensure that you introduce forward bends and inversions to your yoga practice to open and balance the Ajna Chakra.

## SAHASRAHARA (CROWN) CHAKRA – PINEAL GLAND - VIOLET - OM

The Sahasrahara Chakra controls the entire nervous system. The Crown Chakra is a very important Chakra that helps the other six Chakras stay open. However, it is crucial that you balance your Mooladhara or Root Chakra before attempting to balance your Crown Chakra. Be sure to begin with the Root Chakra and work upwards towards the Crown Chakra to help stimulate energy flow and harmony.

The Kundalini Shakti resides in your lower Chakras and the Shiva Shakti resides in your upper Chakras. The Kundalini is waiting to meet its Shiva. But the activation and balance of the Chakras has to be done slowly and properly. The Chakra energies need to be moved higher gently to realise the richness and perfection of life. Do not rush the process because the body energies are strong and should not get disoriented.

A balanced Crown Chakra stands for complete Oneness. You feel oneness for animate and inanimate objects, feel oneness of the Universe. The sense of bounds and separation dilutes completely. Once the Crown Chakra gets activated, you become extremely compassionate, kind, and forgiving. Your motive in life no longer remains solely about fulfilling your passions and desires but also about serving others. Through serving others, you learn to serve yourself.

**Exercises for balancing the Sahasrahara:**

**Exercise 1**

Any form of Meditation or Meditating on the Crown Chakra is best for the activation of the Sahasrahara Chakra. You can also meditate through any other technique. You can focus on your breath, focus on an image – imaginary or real – or simply empty your mind completely and sit in emptiness. What is most important is to connect through the Crown Chakra to the limitless source of energy that lies dormant in your system.

**Exercise 2**

Chanting of 'Om'. This chant causes energy to gather and flow upward and outward. OM is the mantra of acceptance and assent. It helps you to accept your higher self and allow energy to flow openly and freely through you. The chant also helps gather your inward energy and prepare it for moving upwards from the lower Chakras.

**Exercise 3**

Gently tap your Crown area with the tips of your fingers, moving the hands from side to side. This exercise helps awaken the Sahasrahara Chakra. Any posture that brings the crown of the head to the floor such as the fish pose or *Matsyasana* can also help stimulate the Sahasrahara.

**Exercise 4**

Sometime during the week, turn off the TV and all gadgets and open yourself to the sounds of the Universe. Take nature walks or mountain hikes to reconnect to the Universe. Keep a dream journal to write down your dreams and imaginations. Carry a gemstone that resonates with you. Violet or clear gemstones like quartz crystal, diamond or amethyst are recommended for activating the Crown Chakra.

*"Getting in touch with unmet needs is important to the healing process."*

— **Marshall B. Rosenberg**

# CHAPTER 14
## POSITIVE BALANCE - SATIATING THE 6 NEEDS

---◆◆◆---

It might be tough for most of us to comprehend and relate to, but there are a few universal truths that dictate all human behaviour. One such truth is that each of us humans is driven by **6 core needs** that form the base for all our actions, choices, motivations and decisions. Psychological studies have proved that no matter what race, sex, or religion you belong to, no matter where you are born or how you are raised, these six basic needs and how you go about satiating them, controls your fundamental behaviour and determines how you prioritize actions and decisions throughout life.

Consciously or unconsciously, through all our actions, each of us is constantly striving to satiate one or more of these 6 core needs. As unbelievable as it may sound, each of us has absolutely the same needs, but how we value those needs, in what order we prioritize them and the approach we follow to satiate them, determines the direction of our life.

Before I go into the topic in depth, let me lay out the 6 core needs:

**1. Certainty -** The need to feel safe, secure, stable and comfortable.

**2. Variety -** The need for change, stimulation, thrill and challenge.

**3. Significance -** The need to feel important, valued and respected.

**4. Love and Connection** - The need to share love and feel loved, to connect with others.

**5. Growth -** The need for growth (personal, professional and spiritual), progress and enrichment of character and spirit.

**6. Contribution -** The need to share, to contribute in whatever capacity and help others.

Now, you may assume that these needs are complementary for creating a more peaceful, happy and contented life. But in reality, these 6 needs essentially dictate our behavioural traits, our values, belief systems and our approach to people, relationships and life itself.

None of these needs can be or should be done away with or shut off. In fact, meeting these needs is a crucial step towards having more harmony in your lives and relationships.

But the most important aspect that has to be managed is how we try to approach and fulfill these needs. There are negative and harmful ways or positive and empowering ways to meet each of these 6 needs. Unfortunately, many people I interact with satiate their needs through unhealthy and unsustainable habits, leading to frustration, anxiety, stress, and even depression. Only when we are able to align our needs with our values, will peace of mind and contentment exist.

Let's try and assess the positive and negative approaches to satiate each need.

## 1. Certainty

**Healthy approach:** Creating beneficial routines, setting positive belief systems, developing consistency, controlling fears, having a cheerful disposition, engaging in activities that you enjoy, gaining information and knowledge, being organized, expecting positive behaviour from yourself, optimistic thinking.

**Unhealthy approach:** Becoming obsessive or compulsive about habits and routines, hoarding money, depending on relationships to make you comfortable or stable, being overly protective, unhealthy eating, repeated negative behaviour for assertion, control over other people and things, fanatic preparation for the worst.

## 2. Variety

**Healthy approach:** New explorations, meeting challenges, taking intelligent professional risks, learning new things, trying new foods, travelling, finding new hobbies and passions, engaging in stimulating conversations, watching movies, playing different games or sports, reading books, meeting new people.

**Unhealthy approach:** Unintelligent high-risk activities, alcohol and drugs, self-sabotage, harming the self physically or mentally, negative thinking, picking fights, cheating in relationships.

## 3. Significance

**Healthy approach:** Getting popularity and distinction in healthy ways, developing a positive personality, expressing your uniqueness to the world, accomplishing personal and professional goals, developing a unique sense of style, identifying with a purpose, seeking out meaning for life and for your own existence.

**Unhealthy approach:** Trying to poke fun at others to become popular, tearing down others, committing violent acts to gain attention, developing a negative identity, attaching to negative thoughts and assessments, using other people to gain social status, unwanted flattering, lying to impress, rape, murder, war.

## 4. Love

**Healthy approach:** Caring, sharing, openness, intimacy, becoming a part of healthy organizations, teams and groups, developing compassion towards all, spending time in nature, cultivating an understanding of the theory of oneness, healthy sex, healthy physical affection, exchanging gifts, expressing words of love towards yourself and others, performing acts of service, being supportive and non-judgmental, spending quality time with family and friends, caring for pets, connecting with yourself, developing spirituality.

**Unhealthy approach:** Dominating, trying to attract negative attention and sympathy, self-sacrificing, joining gangs, unhealthy sexual interactions, seeking out pity by being sick or having problems consistently, becoming accident-prone so others will pay attention, people-pleasing, causing others to feel as if they need you.

## 5. Growth

Healthy approach: Taking on challenges, learning from others, respecting differences, improvising, improving upon your current situation, following your dreams, being open to change, developing new outlook to problems, working out solutions that help you grow, listening to other people and adopting sensible advice.

**Unhealthy approach:** Pushing yourself too hard whether in personal or professional situations, taking on detrimental challenges, always stuck in problems without finding constructive solutions, not listening openly to other people, not considering sane advice, letting things get to the breaking point before improving them, trying to expand your own agenda.

## 6. Contribution

**Healthy approach:** Random acts of kindness, warm words, small compliments to loved ones or strangers, thank-you notes, useful gifts, attaching to social causes, becoming a part of things you believe in, helping others to make them feel better, a larger vision of love and peace, giving just because it brings joy, joining causes which carry out a solution, volunteering time and skill to a charitable organization, making a donation.

**Unhealthy approach:** Distorted intent while helping others, trying to build a better situation by acting in unhealthy ways towards others, focusing on the problem rather than a solution, joining causes which perpetuate the problem, contributing for self-fame rather than help.

I would sum up this chapter with a small take-away. Need is something that implies a sense of lacking something. However, the 6 human needs are something you cannot do without. Even the most enlightened beings have had the same needs – however, they simply perfected the art of meeting those needs in healthy ways, without expectation, without dependence. Now it is for you to observe how you are currently meeting these 6 needs and how you can replace a few unhealthy ways with healthier ways of meeting those same needs. Once you learn to satiate your needs in a positive way, you will no longer feel a sense of lack, and your personal, professional and spiritual lives will glide along beautifully. Remember, you already are what you are looking for in other people.

*"What shares the purpose of the Universe shares the purpose of its Creator. Try then to look on all things with love, appreciation and open-mindedness."*

— **Anonymous**

# CHAPTER 15
## ALIGNING WITH THE COSMOS

—————— ❖ ——————

Most of us often complain that the Universe does not respond to our calling. We feel as if everything in the Universe is working against us. That we are victims for whom nothing seems to be going right. We keep getting into situations that make us feel low and despondent and this in turn takes a toll on our physical and mental state of being.

So, it would seem rather unbelievable if I say that each of us has the power to make what we want of our lives. We are all capable of pulling together Universal forces to work with us, or rather in tandem with our thoughts and actions. Yes, it is truly possible, provided we are ready to work towards it consciously.

Let me simplify and explain how. I am sure we all

remember the powerful one liner from the Star War Series, **'May the Force be with you'**. Hollywood producer George Lucas weaved into his epic Star Wars saga an exploration of the workings of "The Force" or, simply put, the energy cycle.

Scientifically it has been proven that the human body is a conglomerate of densely-packed energy cells which have their own distinctive vibration. This stands true for each and every element in the Universe as well. Everything in the Universe is also made up of energy. Even a rock's energy vibration is moving constantly. Nothing is still. Each being, every animal, every tree, each element of the Universe is connected to an infinite pool of Universal Energy.

Everything in creation is a form or expression of this energy, including our thoughts and feelings. Our energy is guided by consciousness. So when we have different thoughts and emotions, they generate waves of energy that actually influence what is occurring on the physical plane of reality.

Our beliefs affect what actually occurs in our body. When we are happy, energy flows freely and our body is likely to remain healthy. However, when we have chronic stress and unpleasant thoughts and feelings, our energy flow becomes disturbed and disrupted, and we may develop illness. Just as an electrical appliance can't function well if there is too weak or too strong a current of electricity, our body will have problems operating when there is an imbalance in the subtle energy flow.

The body's energy is comprised of consciousness and awareness. When you learn how to harness and control self-awareness, you can in fact control the experiences you choose to bring into your life.

As surprising as it may sound, the Universe is reading your vibration, each and every second, and reacting accordingly. The most potent and powerful frequency or vibration emerges from your thoughts. Thoughts cause a change in the energy field around you, and it ripples, touching everything. These ripples shift a part of the massive omnipresent energy field. Everything of course ripples back in reaction, sending back your emotions and thoughts to you, all multiplied. If you send out positive and good vibrations, the "boomerang" comes back to you with positive events and positive "coincidences". The same goes for negative emotions or thoughts like anger or hate. The "boomerang" catches up sooner or later and gives you more negative experiences or events. Cosmic energy keeps flowing, without judgment. It is for you to decide whether you want to connect to the flow of this loving energy by positive thinking and action. If you do decide to invite positive universal energy into your life, here are some practical suggestions on how you can rekindle your relationship with the cosmos.

## ASSESS AND RESTRICT THE NEGATIVE
## ENERGY WITHIN YOU

—❧◦❧◦❧—

Do you complain, all the time or just sometimes? Do you often discuss what's wrong in the world more than what's right? Like the 'terrible' weather, 'horrible' traffic, 'ineffective' government or 'unsupportive' in-laws? Do you criticize a lot? Do you mostly blame situations for your mental/ physical state of being? Do you feel like a victim? Are you grateful for all that is or only when things finally start going right for you?

If you answer most of these questions truthfully, you will be shocked to realise how your mind is playing truant every moment, trying to bog you down with negativity.

Mostly in straining situations, the mind sparks off a small negative thought. Slowly you start fuelling this negative thought by looking at more and more things to complain about. This could be in a relationship, a professional setup or just a simple life situation. You also tend to attract the wrong people into your life who aggravate your negativity.

Firstly, it requires a lot of courage to be honest to yourself and assess the level of negativity within you to find ways to counter it. Find a quiet space and look inside. The solution begins with self-awareness.

Remember that positive cosmic energy is all around you. You just need to tap into this positive pool and start harnessing it to alter your thought process. The big difference will come from attitude. It is not unnatural to have negative thoughts. Each of us, including me, has negative thoughts that pop up time and again. The trick lies in countering each negative thought/ argument by thinking about some positive aspect of the person/ situation/ setup that you are dealing with. This will reduce the negativity that keeps building up.

Ensure that each time you feel that everything is going wrong, immediately shift the thought to something that has gone absolutely right or is going absolutely right in life. The mind will slowly begin to alter the thought process and you will be able to gather more and more positive energy around you. Do not try and block a negative thought, because it will strike back sometime. Just make sure to counter it with a solid positive thought. Along the way, be grateful for what is happening, both good and bad. Think of how life situations could have been way tougher than they are. Learn to celebrate the beauty of each moment, each experience, each small achievement, and you will surely begin to invite more positive energy into your life.

## LIMIT SELF-CRITICISM AND DOUBT

One of the toughest fights beyond external situations will have to be with the self-talking Ego mind. Most of us struggle with negative thinking and judgment of the self. 'I can never get things right'. 'Nothing good is happening to me'. 'Nothing good will ever happen to me'. 'I will never find the right job.' 'I will never be happy with my life partner'. These are just some statements that the Ego mind must have thrown up at you some time or the other. Sadly, the Ego mind is really loud. Sometimes it can be harmful, filling you with misguidance and doubt. It can actually make you believe that you are meant to suffer and do not deserve to be happy and blissful.

So the most important battle will have to be with the inner self. It is crucial to limit negative self-talk. Disengage from the situation and assess how good/bad your present status is. Take control of your thinking. Live in the moment, not the past or future because both will lead to self-criticism and doubt. Whenever self-doubt rises, calm your mind with the gentle reassurance that you are an important part of this Universe, and positive forces will take care of you. Be grateful for what is. Like in the movie '3 Idiots', keep repeating this assurance firmly to yourself every day, **'All is well and will be well.'**

## KEEP USING POSITIVE AFFIRMATIONS EVERY DAY TO FREE YOURSELF FROM NEGATIVITY

The Ego mind, stressful lives, a fast-paced world, all these are sources of negativity and stress that none of us can completely cut ourselves off from. We need to learn to design 'happy lives' within the present set up of the Universe.

One basic thought that can help you pull through anything is that between all the commotion and hullabaloo, the positive forces of the Universe are always at work, maintaining balance. Believe that there will be phases of negativity, but positivity will finally take over.

As motivation, let me suggest a few daily affirmations that you can keep repeating to make your belief in a positive Universe stronger. You are free to reject what does not appeal to you, but stick to the ones that resonate with you and seem most relevant to your life. In fact, ideally, try and design some of your own. Keep them written, visible and say them out loud every day.

* ✯ My life may be imperfect, but it sure is great.

* ✯ It's okay to have down days. Everyone has them.

✷ Even when I'm dispirited, I will always be grateful.

✷ Every experience is another important learning.

✷ Everything evolves. This will also pass soon.

✷ I can be wrong sometimes. I will willingly accept it.

✷ I have to overcome what's holding me back.

✷ My happiness today is simply the result of my thinking.

✷ Who I spend quality time with matters.

✷ Judgments are a waste of perfect happiness.

✷ I can definitely make the world a happier place.

✷ Each bit that I am doing is worth it.

## STOP WORRYING ABOUT THE JUDGEMENT OF OTHERS

Worrying about what other people think about you can easily get your mind wandering into the negative zone. Feelings of self-doubt, anxiety, and insecurity get triggered the moment you start fearing social judgement. By caring what others think, you are actually allowing others to control your behaviour. Mostly in professional circles, accomplishing anything is going to annoy some people. You can't let them get in your way. Do what matters to you and will matter to you. The less time and energy you spend on image management, the more time you will get for things that really matter. Once you stop trying to impress others, you will be able to express your true self more fully and connect with people, positively, openly and intimately. Theoretically, all of us know we shouldn't worry about others' opinions, but that's easier said than done. So let's analyze a few practical steps to make this a ground reality.

* **Do not assume what others are thinking.** Assumptions can often lead to bad conclusions. You never know what people think unless you give them a chance.

* **Act on what will serve you long-term.** Do not miss an opportunity due to fear of getting a negative reaction. Be willing to take short-term rejections in exchange for what will serve you long-term.

* **Stop judging yourself.** We are mostly afraid of others judging what we judge for ourselves. When we stop judging and accept ourselves

the way we are, we have no need to fear judgments from others.

✴ **Stop judging others.** The more we judge others, the more we think they judge us. It's an ongoing vicious cycle that you need to break. Instead of judging people, think what you can learn from this person. Sometimes all we can learn is how not to be, and that's also a great learning.

✴ **Care about the ones who count.** Care about what important people in your life think, but only those whose opinions you value. Every acquaintance should not get a vote in how you live your life.

✴ **It's not about you.** People's negative reactions are usually about their own experiences, wounds, and perspectives. It's about their own fears and limitations. It has nothing to do with you.

✴ **Focus on what makes you happy.** If you're afraid to do what makes you happy because of what people might think, you're just wasting your time. The more you channel your energy into what will make a difference in your own life, the less you will need others' approval.

## PRACTISE ANY FORM OF MEDITATION THAT APPEALS TO YOU

Meditation is one of the best mediums that will help you align with the positive forces of the Universe. You can start with a short daily practice that for some could also be just relaxing at the end of the day or sitting still in a quiet place. Once your meditative practice strengthens, you will be able to pull in more cosmic energy. Chaotic thoughts will slowly get streamlined and you will be able to gain clarity. Your decision-making capabilities will get sharper and quicker, whether it be in your personal or professional circle. You will feel a sense of calm which will not let you be perturbed with anxiety, fear, worry or stress. Beyond a peaceful mental state, constant meditation will also result in marked improvement in your physical state of being.

## MAKE EFFORT TO CLEANSE YOUR EXTERNAL SPACE

Though much of your effort to connect with the cosmic energy flow will require inner focus, cleansing your external living space of negative energy will be just as important. It is essential to 'De-clutter'. Let go of unneeded stuff and rearrange your furniture to create more space. This is both practical and useful in helping you feel lighter and more positive. You can also use bells and chimes, and natural incense. Once in a day, try to venture outside to a park or open space. Reconnecting with nature can help you open up to the natural flow of the Universe. It will help you disconnect from your regular pace of life.

The key to experiencing harmony and fulfillment in life will lie in choosing to become aware and 'consciously' harmonizing your thought, intention, and actions with the incredible powers of the Universe. You will slowly realize that aligning with the positive forces of the Universe will in fact enable and empower you to begin experiencing what you desire. This change will also reflect as events, conditions and circumstances which you will experience in each and every area of life. Cosmic energy will help in healing you from inside out and heal your mental, physical, and spiritual self. Once you heal your unconscious mind, your circumstances and your reality will change.

All things will change when YOU change within. **The Power lies within You!!!**

*"In all chaos there is a cosmos,*
*in all disorder a secret order…"*

— **Carl Jung**

# CHAPTER 16
## THE HIDDEN ORDER

W̶e are living in a world order where each one of us is forced to be driven by logic and reasoning. We are taught to question, to analyse, to scrutinise more than to believe. So it is not surprising that the miracles of the Universe often escape our human vision.

Rarely do we sense the beauty and marvel in the 'Hidden Order' that exists in the Universe. It is nearly impossible for the human mind to fathom how the Universe brings together infinite little elements that complement one another and create an immense mechanism where every particle is always in its proper place.

With our methodical minds, most of us do recognize an explicit order, photosynthesis, the water cycle or the seasons of the year, but there is also an implicit order, hidden from our eyes and unexplainable by reason, that remains unnoticed. Imagine the earth moving on its axis day in and day out or each planet remaining in its own orbit and not falling off. Well, the energy of the Universe is actually pulling together all of these miracles. In fact, each one of us is also unknowingly playing an integral part in maintaining this order.

Though each of us is unique and experiences life in different ways, at the root we are all interconnected. Our thoughts and dreams mingle with the thoughts and dreams of everyone else to create what we term 'Universal Consciousness'. But with our lack of knowledge, understanding and belief in this universal order, for our probing minds, this is all extremely hard to digest.

So let me try and explicate this Universal Truth in a logical way so more of us can relate.

Famous physicist Albert Einstein has clearly stated that "everything is energy". The entire world of matter, everything we know, our 5 senses, our brains and the table we sit at for a meal, is really just energy. This energy gathers in various numbers and patterns of movement to create the brain or the table. This stands true for each object in the universe, physical objects, animals and humans. Every bit of matter in the universe, at its core, is only energy.

Each individual is also a mass of energy. Collectively when all human energies come together, they form a big energy pool that generates Universal Consciousness. Each human is just a manifestation of this Consciousness.

Transformational change can happen not only within us but around us too if we realize that though each of us is distinct, we are not separate. We are charged and driven by the omnipresent energy of the Universe which is like a flowing river that connects each soul and object in its course.

Our sense of separateness is only an illusion created by our personality ego. The Ego centers around and focuses on what the individual sees and feels about himself, without much consideration for the emotions or thoughts of others. Although the awareness of Ego is essential, one has to gently tame this Ego from overpowering all thought and action. It is also crucial to become aware and learn to separate the collective self, which is happy, ever thoughtful, caring and tolerant from self-centered ego in order to respect the larger order of the Universe where every soul is linked through vibrational energy.

Importantly, like all other energy sources, the ceaseless flow of Universal energy also carries within it, negative and positive charge. So like a magnet, whatever energy you pull from the

Universe keeps coming towards you with greater intensity. The focus an individual lays on a thought, whether negative or positive, gets fuelled multifold. This is what is happening with negative thinking. With rising complexities of the modern world and distressing happenings, mistrust, pessimism and doubt are mounting, blocking positive energies to flow through and improve the overall feel of life. Most of us, unknowingly or unconsciously are intensifying negativity by focusing on conflict, problems, sickness, anger and hatred. We fail to counter this by positive thought, looking at the good acts happening around or counting our small little blessings every day.

While we survive in this world order, it is absolutely impossible that we do not become insecure or cynical at some point. But the solution lies in countering any negative thought with positive peaceful thinking. Believe it or not, if all of us learn the importance of being in a peaceful loving state inside, our energy vibrations can impact the external world around us, and influence how others feel as well. In fact, operating from a place of peace within oneself can lead to a very different experience, not only for the person emitting these emotions but also for those around them. It is a proven fact that positive vibrational frequencies have the power to change physical reality. Since we are all interconnected through energy flow, together, we have the collective ability to cause change through positive thought.

In the order of the Universe, each one of us has access to knowledge, known and unknown. We have access to an infinite energy source from where nothing is impossible, we have access to limitless creativity from the Universe. All that is needed is to raise consciousness levels and connect to the eternal source.

When you learn to connect and become aware and conscious, you control the experiences you choose to bring into your life. 'What you think, you create!' Each of your thoughts flies out like a bolt of energy into the universe to bring the result of that thought back into your life, like a mirror reflecting back to you. Whether that thought is good or bad - you create it into your own reality. Remember here that the Law of Attraction is also at work. You are constantly attracting things to come into your life. So it is important to learn the skill of rearranging your energy patterns so that you can attract positive thoughts and energies from the Universe.

In fact, in true terms, it is no exaggeration to say that you can create your ideal reality because you are already connected to everything you want. You can experience happiness, true love, perfect health, abundance, wealth and anything else you intend.

All you have to do is bring yourself into vibrational harmony with the Universe and work around the creative power of your thoughts.

I have observed out of practical experience that most of us get accustomed to focusing on problems, worries, fears, and what we lack. We keep thinking about how bad our job is, and it keeps getting worse. We worry about our health and disease, and that's what we attract...more ill-health. Focus on what we term bad luck, and that is just what we receive. We constantly focus on the results we are getting today, and never on what we want the results to be.

We have to realize that our thinking controls our results. We need to be completely and totally focused on the results we want and not on the ones we currently have. We have to be grateful for what is happening, both good and bad. We have to focus on solutions instead of problems. It is equally important to understand that feeling low or negative is a normal thing that will happen with all the ups and downs that life has to offer. But rather than just wallowing in those feelings or thoughts, we need to hold the responsibility of pulling ourselves away from negative feelings and take immediate or long-term corrective action.

Sadly, almost all of us tend to wait for positivity to happen to us, but that never happens because we never invest energy into focusing or trying.

Instead of waiting, we have to master the skill of pulling positivity into our lives ourselves. Just as a push, let me put forth a few practical suggestions that can work towards amplifying positive thinking and help connect with the infinite energy pool, bringing about transformational change in thought patterns.

Before thinking of any change, acknowledge and accept the fact that there is a Universal Force which is omnipresent, omnipotent and omniscient. Be ready to draw energy from this force.

Realize that within the energy of the Universe is creativity that you can tap into and make real whatever you have the power to visualize

Learn to be kind and forgiving. Remember that kindness will benefit you more than the other person.

Limit Ego talk that leads to doubt and negative
self-judgment. "Nothing good will ever happen
to me," "I could never do that," "I'll never find the
right job." "I'm a horrible person," "I don't deserve
happiness" - cut out all these negative affirmations
and replace them with positive ones.

Counter each negative thought with a positive one.
Stop complaining about everything around.
Instead, count your little blessings every day.
You will begin to see a marked shift
in your thought pattern.

Be Loving. Do not keep judging, do not be angry
or resentful for long. Momentary bouts of irritation
and anger are fine but do not let that affect all your
thoughts and actions. Respect that each individual
is living his own experience but is connected to you
in the larger universal picture.

Focus on the beauty of life and celebrate each moment. This will give you reason to smile, even in the worst of situations.

Remember that there is an infinite pool of energy out there that you can draw from. Gently rearrange your energies to pull in the abundant positivity flowing through the Universe.

Try and meditate every day, in your own way. This can be through prayer, yoga, exercise, play or just simple deep breathing, whatever suits you and can be done comfortably. This will help you observe and connect to universal energies.

Trust me, the process of changing your thought patterns will not be a simple one. It's like changing old habits. You will have to keep struggling, trying and failing but over a period of time, you will start enjoying a different perspective to life with a 'new, transformed you'. Once you begin to attract positive energy into your life, it will harmonize and balance your connection with the cosmos.

As I travel across the globe for my lectures and healing sessions, it has been heartening to notice a slow shift of many, especially the younger generation, to more broad-based belief systems and their efforts to recognize and respect the hidden order of the Universe. I have observed a gradual rise in consciousness, where individuals have started viewing the world holistically rather than as a collection of disassociated parts. It is stimulating to meet young individuals who are conscious and serious about remodelling the wider world order or finding comprehensive solutions to global issues

At the risk of sounding over-optimistic, I believe that maybe, we are gradually heading towards a spiritual revolution which will pave the way for higher global consciousness, encouraging each of us to move beyond established separations, and open up new approaches to living life meaningfully and peacefully in a constantly evolving universe.

*'Magic happens when you tell the Universe
what you want it to do for you, Miracles happen
when you ask how you can be of service to the Universe.'*

# CHAPTER 17
## MAGIC HAPPENS

— ◆◆◆ —

I believe in Magic. I believe in fairies and fairytales. And I am sure most of you believe in Magic too. Do you remember getting enchanted and amazed by life's little wonders as kids? The flight of birds and the airplane, the bubbles that came out of a soap ring, and the colourful rainbow that popped out from nowhere once in a while, all seemed to have some magical quality about them. But as we began to grow up, we were conditioned to think that believing in magic was foolish and wasteful.

Then as adults, caught up in analyzing, problem-solving, and simply surviving, the charm and aura that magic held back then completely faded. Rationale and logic started to overtake thinking and the heart forgot how to believe, to dream and to appreciate the miracles of the Universe.

In fact, about 30 years back, when I was struggling and striving, and the ups and downs of life were shaking me up, I was in the same phase. It was nearly impossible for me to believe that I could create the magical life I desired. I struggled to find some meaning in life, not knowing who to orient my questions to. There were varied thoughts that perplexed my mind - about my personal journey, my professional success, my family life, my health, and my kids. I could barely look around and appreciate the beauty and magic that life had veiled.

However, I have to admit that unconsciously, my belief in some positive power within and outside of me kept me looking out for miracles and they did come my way.

My volatile journey of self-exploration has helped me unravel some magical truths that I would want to share with all my readers. I learnt that despite all the struggles and challenges, there are thousands of reasons to find joy and magic in life and in every moment, if you so intend. Miracles are happening everywhere, all around us. The only thing we need to do to notice them is to live in 'awareness'. Magic will reveal itself when you learn to celebrate every moment, here and now. I would in fact move a step further to say that each one of us has the power to 'Create Magic' in our lives, provided we believe in ourselves, we believe in the power of the Universe and in the power within us. We can find magic in the mundane if we decide to look for it.

Let me ask you a simple question. How many of you feel *enchanted* right now? How many of you have the instinct to look at your surroundings, and appreciate the beauty in little things? Probably not too many.

Have you ever wondered why we never feel enchanted by our lives? It's simply because as we grow up, we fail to approach life with a sense of joy, wonderment and the spark and creativity of a child. Bogged down by mundane activities, we cease to take time out and delight in the simple charm of creation – a baby smiling, a puppy prancing around or a lovely, colourful flower blooming.

The Magic of life is really about finding newness and excitement in day-to-day activities and being open and ready to get enchanted by our own mundane life. The process is surely not an easy one. Initially you might feel silly and childish to keep finding magic in everything around but once you get accustomed to the habit of exulting in the mundane, you will strengthen the power of positive thought and be able to co-create something wonderful in your life. As you begin to acknowledge and appreciate the little miracles around, the Universe will also conspire with you and support you in what you wish to create. It will work in synchronicity with your thoughts and pull more positive energies into your daily life. That is the power of Magic. That is the beauty of Miracles.

Let me quote an interesting saying by Einstein that I came across during my reads. He says "There are only two ways to live your life. One is as though nothing is a miracle. The other is as though everything is a miracle." I would rather go with the latter and find reasons to make life more interesting and exciting rather than merely coasting through it.

I have to admit here that while there is no sure-shot formula to suddenly making life miraculous in a week or month, there are a few things you can do and gradually pave the way to unlock Magic in your life. You can start right now with these basic tips, no matter how busy you are.

## TRUST THAT 'MAGIC' EXISTS

Be childlike. Imagine yourself in a world of amazing possibilities, where you are capable of doing anything your heart desires. Keep your mind open when it comes to looking for magic in everyday life. Believe that you can find magic even in the most mundane activity, like driving to work. Switch up your route, play music that you love, pay attention to the things you see - sometimes even billboards, road signs or amusing messages behind buses and trucks.

Trust that magic exists for you, no matter how old you are, and you will slowly begin to experience its charm.

## STAY FOCUSED ON THE PRESENT

One of the biggest reasons we do not see magic in our lives any more is because we are not really in the present moment. Most of our thoughts and actions are driven either by the pain of the past or anxiety about the future. In the process, we overlook the amazing experiences right in front of us. It is perfectly fine to think about the past or future but it is not ok to sink in the thought. Again I would suggest that you draw inspiration from a kid. Whenever a child takes up any activity, he is so immersed in it that there is no sense of the past or future. All awareness is focused on the present moment and on the current activity. This is a quality each of us needs to imbibe. To stay focused on the present. Observe, admire and appreciate what is around. Do whatever needs to be done today and now to make life meaningful and blissful.

## LET 'LOVE' OVERPOWER ALL EMOTION

Give love. Share love. Speak love.

In fact, as a first step, practise loving yourself -

your physical self, your mental and emotional self. Then practise spreading that love onto others. Begin to look for reasons to love someone for their positive qualities, ignoring their flaws, and expand the circle of love. Look for every opportunity to reflect love back at the world. Replace fear- or obligation-driven behaviour with love-motivated behaviour, especially towards family and friends. Also understand that Love is both sides of the experience - praise and reprimand, support and challenge, being lifted up and put down simultaneously. When you honour this balance, your outlook towards giving and receiving love will stand totally transformed. Make love the place from where amazing opportunities and experiences will emerge. Be a transmitter of love so the universe can work through you and manifest whatever your heart imagines.

## ACKNOWLEDGE MIRACLES

The Universe is a treasure trove of Miracles that are happening every single minute, each day. From the miracle of birth to the earth spinning on its axis, causing a brand-new day, nature shows us miracles all the time. Even in our daily lives, many miracles go unnoticed. From the fresh air we breathe to the warmth of the sun, from the food we eat to the water that hydrates, we have magical stuff all around. But sadly, most of us tend to overlook these miracles altogether. Magic happens when you begin to recognize and acknowledge the miracles and blessings that surround you. You need to notice and appreciate the special gifts that grace your life - family, relationships, friends and love. When anything good happens in your life, even the smallest good, don't just brush it aside. Loudly acknowledge it and thank the Universe. Be sure that this good will multiply tenfold. Learn to bring some magic to the world by creating miracles of your own. Do something delicate and wonderful for someone else. Give someone who is feeling down a warm hug. Send someone colourful flowers once in a while. Pass someone a compliment or a gentle smile. Buy small gifts and deliver them randomly to friends. If you have the capacity, try and help someone struggling with financial trouble. There are a myriad of ways to create your own miracles, and the magic is that the more miracles you create, the more you would want to create. Your small little miracles will create a ripple and people will tend to pass them on with new miracles for others.

## ENJOY THE SIGHTS, SOUNDS AND SMELLS OF NATURE

Open your eyes to the joy and beauty of nature. Listen carefully to the melody that comes with the sounds that surround you each day. Stop to smell the wonderful fragrance of blooming roses, or enjoy the rich, wonderful aroma of a dish being cooked back home. The world we live in is full of amazing sights, sounds and smells. Appreciate and admire the natural beauty that surrounds you. Whether it is by basking in the warm sunlight or soaking in the sight of cotton clouds at sunset, all these experiences can bring you a new appreciation of the natural majesty held within this world, and evoke magic in all your senses.

## VISUALISE YOUR DREAMS

What is the vision you hold for your life? Where do you see your personal or professional life going? What do you really believe in? Embrace it. Cultivate it and let it turn real. Give yourself permission to dream big and then get going to make that dream a reality. Set an intention. Make a vision board or just write out your intentions on a piece of paper and burn it. Let the Universe know what you want to make of your life. It is perfectly ok to dream of a bigger house, a better relationship or more comfort, but setting a wider intention of more love, abundance, friendship or happiness can work wonders. Also remember not to lose hope if you do not see immediate results. The Universe admires patience. Just keep your dream alive and visualise it come true. There is nothing more magical than envisioning the life your soul craves for.

## GET CURIOUS

Feeling a bit uninspired and stuck in your mundane routine? Well, it's time to get curious. Believe me, it's a brilliant feeling to reconnect with your inner child and explore new interesting facts. As a start, read up and learn about topics you have been curious to know about. Try new foods, travel to new places or catch a new hobby. It might also be a good change to join some community activity. Shake up and put the spark back into life. The change will be magical.

## PLAY!

Let loose, jump around, just have fun! Once in a while, it is essential to relive your childhood and unwind. Have fun in whatever way you love. Go for an adventure trip with your gang, hang around for a chat and coffee with friends, spend quality time with your family and kids. Play board games, card games or enjoy more activity-driven sports. Learn to relax and luxuriate and watch how it refines every area of your life for the better.

## CONNECT

Try and connect with like-minded individuals who share positive vibes and energy. Whenever you meet someone, try and connect with them at a level where your energies meet. Join workshops, sessions or any platform that will help you meet like-minded people. Build a community of individuals who can share, connect, and celebrate one another, enriching lives and creating a magnificent ripple effect across the world.

## CHANGE YOUR PERSPECTIVE

Rather than looking at life from an angle of fear, apprehension, doubt and distrust, shift your focus to expect the best in life. No anxiety. No worry. Just focus on the positives you see around. Lean on the sense of magic and wonder that you had as a child. The world will be filled with amazing opportunities and when you expect the best, that's exactly what you will receive.

Once you learn to step up the Magic quotient, Life will not merely 'happen' to you, but you will have the power to co-create it, working with the dynamic intelligence of the Universe. You will have the power to manifest your thoughts and desires and receive all that your soul craves for, easily and effortlessly. However, you will have to keep in mind a few basics that will deepen your manifesting capabilities and help transform your life in miraculous ways.

## RELAX AND BE PRESENT

The infinite source of power is here and now. The entire Universe is happening only in this moment. Being present in the moment is one of the most essential and basic keys to manifesting. Once your mind is free from distracting thoughts about the past and future, then you can activate magical manifesting powers. You will need to learn how to relax and slow down so mental chatter can lessen and you can manage, slot and organize your thoughts better. You also need to master slowing down your breathing and the movement of your body. This practice will create more depth, relaxation and awareness in your being.

## AIM AT SOME 'STILL' MOMENTS EVERY DAY

There are deadlines to meet and commitments to keep. With the fast pace of life in changing times, our ability to concentrate and focus has gone down drastically. Our brains are working 24/7, leaving no scope for peaceful thinking. There is constant chatter in the mind each moment of the day. It is here that a meditative practice can help. Each day, very consciously, pull time out and train the mind to be still, even if it is for a few moments. Practice focusing on one single thing, the easiest being your breath. Strengthen the mind and learn to concentrate without distraction. Manifesting will be easier once you learn to maintain focus and be calm and peaceful on the inside.

## THINK POSITIVE AND ACCOMMODATE SETBACKS

Extreme attachment to the outcome whenever you take a step towards fulfilling your dream is a drawback that can hamper the magical process of manifestation. It is amazing to visualize, imagine and envision your dream, but attachment to each stage of the process and analysis of each result will lead to distress. Instead, having a deep, positive, open connection with your desired outcome without being overly attached to it, is one of the greatest hidden keys to manifesting it. Let the Universe know that you whole-heartedly love the dream that you want to manifest in your life. Do not get disheartened if you do not see things manifesting as you intend. Just stay positive and devoted towards manifesting your dream.

## BE GRATEFUL

Never underestimate the power of a simple 'thank you' to another person or to the Universe. Gratitude is the foundation upon which magic is born. Be grateful for every small blessing and celebrate each moment of happiness and peace. Be thankful for whatever the Universe has brought your way. Cultivating an attitude of gratitude will make your outlook towards life hopeful and positive. It will slowly begin to act like a magnet to attract more incredible experiences and opportunities into your life.

## HAVE FAITH

Though this might sound like a religious concept to many, I do not mean having faith in the religious sense of the word. By Faith, I mean believing in a higher, omnipresent, intelligent power that is inside and outside of you. You can term it God, the Universe or the Eternal Source. Build a conscious personal connection with this sacred, intelligent source that is everywhere you are. Give yourself a special time each day to be still, quiet and connect with this higher power. When you feel some form of connection, ask for the blessing of bringing your desired goal into form. Do not forget to pray for yourself and others. Pray, not for getting something in return but for peace, strength and hope. If you work towards fulfilling your dream with all sincerity, you will be able to manifest the most amazing results.

## HELP SELFLESSLY

Look for opportunities to help others in some way. Help needn't always be financial. You can serve someone with your time, your talents and your intelligence or simply with your love. **Serve freely, without expectation.** Try to help one person each day. Improve someone's life in small, little ways. Give when you aren't asked. The universe is observant. It will reciprocate your service to others with something magical.

## DO NOT WORRY ABOUT JUDGEMENTS AND PERCEPTIONS

Never fall into the trap of judging others or yourself. Do not brand people or slot them into categories. Each individual is unique and holds his own charm. Situations and circumstances might drive certain behaviour, but when you start passing judgements based on that behaviour, you block positive, intelligent thinking. You need to learn the importance of exercising empathy at work and in life, so you begin to connect with others and try to understand their circumstances and the burdens they face. This move will open up compassion and love towards others and yourself. Help find solutions to problems, whether your own or that of others. The universe uses compassion and love as fertilizer to allow your life to bloom. Also, relinquish your need for external approval. Be your own judge. You are the best judge of your worth, and your goal is to discover infinite worth in yourself, no matter what anyone else thinks.

## FORGIVE

The universe can only bring you love when the wounds of pain and anger have healed. You must forgive to allow healing and love to envelop your life. Forgive anyone and everyone who has caused you pain in the past, more for yourself than for them. If you do not forgive, the universe will have no capacity to bring you what you deserve. Let go of emotional turmoil, bitterness and hurt. Let go of the past. Let go of painful experiences. Universal energy cannot flow if you have a wall of negative vibrations around you. Rid yourself of all negativity. Be like the sky. Allow feelings, experiences and desires to float past but do not grab onto them. Even if you've been hurt or betrayed, lower the walls you've built around yourself. Allow loving kindness to soften your heart. Make anger and spite melt away under the potent power of love.

## LOVE YOURSELF

You are worthy of attaining any dream, vision or goal. You have magical potential to make anything happen. Believe in yourself. Drop any neediness for love, acceptance and approval from others and replace it with self-love. Invest time and energy to send yourself loving and appreciative thoughts. You will increase your manifesting ability and power with every loving feeling you have about yourself. Unveil the magic hidden in your own being.

## TRUST THE UNIVERSE

**Have trust in the powers of the Universe. You might not know the "how", the "when" or the "why" of your miraculous life journey right now.** Just keep going. Trust that you will know the steps to take when the time is right. Also understand that once you are committed to your dream, you will be supported by the universe 100% of the time. Resources, time, money, and contacts will arrive exactly when you need them. Friends, coaches and mentors will come in to guide and encourage you when you need it. Be infinitely patient!  Let go of anxiety, disbelief and doubt.  Believe that your goal is on its way.  The Universe will always support what you want and help you achieve it.

## BE OPEN

Reveal your intentions to the Universe but do not keep checking on each step of the process how things will work out. Be open to various manifestations of your intention.  It may not be exactly how you had wished, but it will be what is right for you. The Universe will use its infinite wisdom to point and lead you in certain directions, maybe at times not the ones you understand. Instead of fighting it, go with the flow. Don't fear or close up. Follow the Universe's lead and it will take you exactly where you are to be.

## BE PATIENT

Do not be pushy or set timelines for the Universe to deliver what you request. Be patient and stay committed. Do not lose hope. The Universe will work its way and make things happen. If the time is not right, the Universe might delay the opportunity but it will come together soon. Make space in your life so the Universe can fill it with the things you want.

## EMBRACE YOUR BLISS

Do whatever makes you happy. Show up for the things that matter in your life, the things that you value and the things that you love. Be at the places your heart calls you to. Show up for your passions, dreams, values and people who matter to you. Surround yourself with experiences and people that enrich your soul. Seek and experience continuous moments of joy in your day-to-day life. Raise your vibrations by feeling good. Seek to be in a continuous state of bliss, joy and delight. This is the ultimate secret to manifesting your every wish.

Once you begin to appreciate the universal laws and divine order, even without asking for it, miracles will happen. Your sense of gratitude for the marvellous gift of life will awaken and you will become inspired to live the dream you were created to fulfil. Providence will begin to move with you. The Universe will synchronise its energies with your energy and you will begin to co-create the magical life you desire.

New people and opportunities will unexpectedly come your way, helping you with what you want to achieve. The Universe will open up the path that will lead you to your goal and obstacles will disappear. Your inner wisdom will guide you at each stage. You will expand your thinking and your consciousness to a whole new level which will help you make a positive impact on every person you get in touch with.

Your thoughts and beliefs will comprise of openness, hope, and gratitude, and not fear, resentment or doubt. You will realise that you are not only moving towards your dream but in fact living your dream, at this instant, in this moment. It will all seem like magic, but it's not. It's just that you are creating your new reality. You are transforming into a better being, crafting a peaceful and wonderful life for yourself and all those around you.